Dulcimer Maker

Homer C. Ledford

DULCIMER MAKER

♥

The Craft of
HOMER LEDFORD

♥

R. Gerald Alvey

PHOTOGRAPHS BY
Jerry Schureman

THE UNIVERSITY PRESS OF KENTUCKY

Publication of this book has been assisted by a grant from the National Endowment for the Humanities.

Scholarly publisher for the Commonwealth,
serving Bellarmine College, Berea College, Centre
College of Kentucky, Eastern Kentucky University,
The Filson Club, Georgetown College, Kentucky
Historical Society, Kentucky State University,
Morehead State University, Murray State University,
Northern Kentucky University, Transylvania University,
University of Kentucky, University of Louisville,
and Western Kentucky University.

Editorial and Sales Office: Lexington, Kentucky 40506-0024

Library of Congress Cataloging in Publication Data

Alvey, R. Gerald, 1935-
  Dulcimer maker.

  Includes index.
  1. Appalachian dulcimer. 2. Ledford, Homer,
1927-   . 3. Musical instruments—Makers—Kentucky—
Biography. I. Title.
ML1015.A6A45   1984   787'.942   82-40463
ISBN 0-8131-1447-0

TO THE MEMORY OF WM. HUGH JANSEN

CONTENTS

ILLUSTRATIONS

INTRODUCTION

The Appalachian mountain dulcimer is, in the strictest sense of the term, a folk culture instrument, its construction and use having "taken place within the currency of an oral tradition of music."[1] Although the exact date of the introduction of the Appalachian dulcimer, and its earliest history, are unknown or at best unclear, it was probably not common until the nineteenth century.[2] No similar instrument is traditional to the British Isles; however, several closely allied instruments are traditional to northern Europe—the Swedish *hummel*, the Norwegian *langeleik*, the Icelandic *langspil*, the German *sheitholt*, and the French *epinette des Vosges*—though the dulcimer does not exactly duplicate any of them.[3] Therefore, scholars believe that the dulcimer was developed in this country, probably by settlers from northern Europe.[4] Furthermore, as far as is known, the traditional Appalachian dulcimer has never been a factory-made instrument, rather always the handmade product of the individual craftsman who fashioned it, usually in his own home or workshop.

A plethora of data exist on the Appalachian dulcimer as a folkcraft, as well as discussions of its ethnomusicological aspects. However, comparatively little information has been published concerning the craftsmen who create these folk instruments.[5] Such scholarly neglect is regrettable, as the mountain dulcimer exists only through the artistry and traditions of the individual craftsman, who is a complex individual, motivated by a multiplicity of forces, and whose vitality as a tradition bearer cannot be separated from the strength of the dulcimer tradition itself.[6] As Michael Owen Jones observes, "Research into human behavior must begin and end with human beings and should focus on the individual, for an object cannot be fully understood or appreciated without knowledge of the man who made it, and the traits of one object cannot be explained by reference only to antecedent works of an earlier period from which later qualities allegedly evolved."[7] Agreeing with Jones are a growing number of contemporary folklorists who, although acknowledging the need for theoretical approaches to traditional phenomena, decry the apparent disregard of "individual human beings, who not only carry traditions but originate them, interpret them in a very personal way, and work on them, whether consciously or unconsciously."[8] Reflective of such inattention is the serious dearth of well-documented studies of the folk artist at work.[9]

As an endeavor to provide one well-documented study, and in keeping with the recent trend in folkloristics increasingly to evaluate the significance of biographical data for its influence on tradition, this book discusses the craft of dulcimer making primarily from the perspective of one craftsman: Homer Ledford, of Winchester, Kentucky; the book endeavors to illustrate the manner in which a folk craft is often intricately bound up with the personality and experiences of the craftsman—what H.G. Barnett calls "biographical determinants" of creativity, innovation, and so forth.[10] Utilizing such an approach, the book necessarily examines the relationships between tradition, popular culture, elite culture, and change and innovation as they are reflected in both Homer Ledford's craft and in the man himself. Some discussion of folk culture aesthetics is also included, as Homer does possess a fine sense of aesthetics and incorporates it in the objects he makes.

Central to this study is a conception of culture as a process of learning and acquiring knowledge, and of expressing that knowledge; I see, moreover (as do most folklorists), American society as comprising three main cultural systems: elite culture, popular culture, and folk culture. In essence, of course, "culture" is an abstraction, an analytic category used in endeavors to explain what people do. In other words, "culture" does not exist—rather people simply exist in certain ways; do things; create things; hold values, beliefs, aspirations, and so on. These we call culture, and patterned similarities in these cultural ways of life we call either elite, popular, or folk. Yet it should be understood that the diverse activities of people involved in complex sociocultural processes, such as a man's making and selling dulcimers, are impossible to categorize absolutely in reality; rather they can be categorized only analytically, and no analytic scheme is

capable of compartmentalizing reality into discrete entities—
especially intricate sociocultural processes—in such a way that
categories for discussion are devoid of features discussed under other
categories. Analytic categories, in other words, are not mutually exclusive; rather, they are guidelines to help us understand and appreciate reality.

Concerning folk culture's processes of making things, not only
is there a limited number of folkloristic examinations of the maker
and the object, there is also relatively little folkloristic scholarship
examining such folk culture processes and their relationships with
elite and popular culture, and the roles of creativity, innovation and
change, and aesthetics in such processes. Consequently, I have often
had to rely upon scholars from other disciplines for commentary in
support of my arguments and observations. Moreover, the few folkloristic studies of folk culture processes of making things that do exist
deal primarily with arts and crafts other than dulcimer making. While
such excellent studies as those by Michael Owen Jones, Henry
Glassie, William Ferris, and Charles Joyner all concern folk culture
arts and crafts—and Jones's works especially delve into innovations,
creativity, and aesthetics—only Joyner's study concerns itself exclusively with dulcimer making.[11] I believe that such a dearth of
scholarship indicates a need which I hope this present work will help
to fulfill.

Part I of the book is both a biographical analysis of the cultural
influences on Homer Ledford that helped to shape his life as a traditional musical-instrument craftsman, and an inquiry into the processes through which Homer has developed and perfected his craft.
Part II is a rather detailed presentation of Homer's traditional craft—
how the Ledford dulcimer is constructed, how it is tuned and played,
how it should be cared for and repaired, and related technical matters. Part III is a folkloristic discussion and evaluation of Homer Ledford and his craft, and their place in the history of traditional dulcimer
making in the United States.

Some of the data for this study were collected during two intensive field trips to Kentucky in the summers of 1971 and 1972, while
I was residing in Pennsylvania; many insights were achieved as a
result of intermittent discussions with Homer over several years' ac-
quaintance, dating back to 1967; furthermore, I have resided in
Homer's community (Winchester, Kentucky) for several years and
consequently have become personally acquainted with him. In working with Homer through the years, I have used nearly every conceivable field procedure; nonetheless, insights were often obtained

quite by accident during personal, nonfieldwork visits with the Ledfords.[12] Some tape recordings of my interviews with Homer are to be deposited with the Smithsonian Institution; as a result of my fieldwork, examples of Homer's craftsmanship were presented in one of the Smithsonian's traveling exhibits; and one of Homer's dulcimers has been purchased for the Smithsonian's permanent collection.[13] Quotations from Homer's comments appearing throughout the book are all extracted from my personal interviews with him.

As other folklorists have suggested concerning relationships with folk artists and craftsmen, I have tried to be not a liablity but an asset to Homer. Consequently, I have tried to help him in various ways—by distributing his brochures; through word-of-mouth advertising; by arranging for personal appearances that provide honoraria; by bringing his work to the attention of scholars, museums, and the like; and last, through this book.[14]

To some extent this book represents a compromise between Homer's and my own notions about what it should entail. Homer wanted something less scholarly, and much shorter, to give his customers—a kind of "how to take care of your dulcimer" manual. I thought the book should have been even more thorough, including discussions of Homer's repertoire and musical performances. Still, since such studies will come in the way of articles, I am quite pleased with the more narrow, more specific focus of the book; the orientation is precisely one that will, in combination with other such studies, aid in "the interpretation of the historical evolution of American culture as represented by the material evidence of that culture,"[15] as well as demonstrate how the permanent and influential mark of the individual personality in folk-culture processes has helped not only to perpetuate tradition but also to create it.

I wish to acknowledge my indebtedness to all who helped me with this study, and special thanks go to the following for their encouragement during research: Professor Don Yoder, Professor Kenneth Goldstein, Professor Archie Green, and the staffs of the University of Kentucky and Berea College libraries. A special note of appreciation is for my dear friend, mentor, and colleague, the late Wm. Hugh Jansen; his influence has been indelible, and his presence will be forever remembered. Particular thanks also go to my long-suffering wife, Donna, who read and typed the manuscript, and to the entire Ledford family: Colista, Homer's wife, was very supportive; and Cindy, Homer's daughter, did the sketches and diagrams. The works of award-winning photographer Jerry Schureman have brought the text alive; I am deeply grateful to him.

Although I have actually written and compiled the material herein, in a very real sense this is Homer Ledford's book; it is his story and a presentation of his highly individual yet traditional craft. Homer read the manuscript for accuracy, yet I stand responsible for any errors and for the evaluations and views presented. To Homer, and to those who helped me, goes whatever favorable comment this work may receive.

I
HOMER LEDFORD:
THE MAN AND
THE CRAFTSMAN

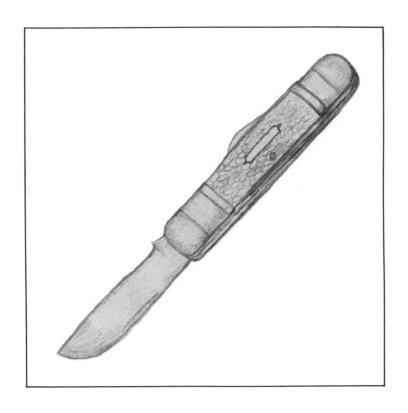

As the loud and lengthy applause from the 200-odd members of the audience subsided, the performer of mountain music, who was seated in the middle of the mountain amphitheater's stage, playing his own homemade instruments, slowly pulled from his right-hand pants pocket a small, well-worn, black-handled pocketknife. With a wry grin, he held it up before his audience and said, "Since I told you these instruments are my own—I made them myself—I just thought you might like to see what my *shop* looks like." The audience laughed at the obvious joke, a laugh mixed with respect, even awe, for the equally obvious craftsmanship and musical quality of the instruments.

The performer was Homer C. Ledford, one of the oldest and finest craftsmen of traditional Appalachian musical instruments in the United States; the year was 1973, and Homer was performing at the eighth annual Kentucky Highlands Folk Festival at Jenny Wiley State Resort Park near Prestonsburg. In the following pages, Homer Ledford's development as an outstanding traditional craftsman will be traced from his boyhood years to the present maturation of his craft. That examination will reveal that while Homer's common practice of showing "his shop" during performances truly reflects how he began—and partially continues—his work, in reality the practice of his craft today is considerably more complicated.

The youngest of four children—two brothers and one sister—Homer C. Ledford was born to a family of Scotch-Irish descent on September 26, 1927, in the rural Tennessee mountain community then known as Ivyton; he spent his early youth—until he left home at age 18—on his father's farm near what is now called Alpine, Tennessee.

Although there were no traditional musical instrument makers either in Homer's family or in the immediate neighborhood, there were several self-taught musicians. Homer recalls that "everyone loved music," and in such an atmosphere his own musical inclinations developed quickly. "I listened to neighborhood boys play guitar, fiddle, and—once in a while—banjo," Homer states, and periodically "the local people congregated at our house for play-parties; we had fiddles, banjos, and guitars, and sometimes even a mandolin; we had singing and buck-wing dancing too."[1] However, as Homer sadly remembers, these gatherings did not long continue, as uninvited drunken ruffians often disrupted them. Homer states that the regular participants "never had hard drink," because for most there were prevailing religious prohibitions against alcohol. The dominant religious groups in Homer's youthful environment were those typical of most southern mountain areas: Baptist, Methodist, Holiness, and other—primarily fundamentalist—Protestant sects.

Because religion was, in general, highly respected by the adults of Homer's childhood, it was a natural consequence that religious music should especially appeal to him. Indeed, it was often through a religion-oriented situation that even nonreligious traditional music was presented. For example, Homer explains that he first became interested in "what is called folk music" while attending high school: "The principal introduced some folk songs into the chapel programs by way of a little songbook.[2] At that time, as a teenager, I really didn't enjoy them very much because I wasn't familiar with them; that is, I had not heard them in my own community, or over the radio, or on wax recordings. Most mountain people are this way: if you don't know something, aren't familiar with it already, you don't accept it readily; it must prove itself." The need for familiarity before acceptance is indeed a trait of many mountain people, whether the "stranger" be a person, a situation, a tangible object, or even, as in Homer's case, a song.[3] In time, however, Homer accepted printed representations of folk songs, even grew to love them, and today includes many in his repertoire.[4] Yet such printed folk songs were not indigenous to Homer's mountain community, not songs everyone grew up with, knew intimately, and played, sang, hummed, or whistled from memory.

Homer cannot recall anyone at all from his youth who might be called a traditional ballad singer and he fully comprehends the folkloristic criteria for that designation. Conversely, nearly everyone knew many religious songs—what Homer now calls "folk hymns"—and these seemed to be perpetually active pieces in everyone's repertoire. On the other hand, not everyone's repertoire included the nonreligious songs then current in the community.[5] In other words, anyone who performed at all played or sang *some* religious pieces, while some performers preferred *only* religious music. Typical, perhaps, was a family Homer remembers who lived in a small house on his father's land; they sang a few religious songs and a great many secular songs, but one female member of the family usually sang only religion-oriented songs, most often "The Little Rosewood Casket," "How Great Thou Art," or "Tell Mother I'll Be There." Later, this same woman, who owned a Stella guitar that she often used to accompany her religious singing, helped Homer when he taught himself to play the guitar. Of course, the bent for religious music in Homer's early environment was perpetuated through regular and frequent church attendance by nearly everyone in the community.

Contemporary secular music entered Homer's community by various routes. Perhaps the least frequent and most irregular performances, but by no means the least influential, were those by itinerant musicians. "When I was a boy," Homer remembers, "there was a very good fiddler and a guitar player who traveled all over the country, and they came to our house every year; Bob Collins was the fiddler's name, and his friend's was Skeets McDonald. They played for their food and lodging; they might even stay a week; and we would have people come in and they would play for everyone, and some of the local people would play, too." Needless to say, those itinerants must have been effective agents for the dissemination and perpetuation of both established and innovative music.

Concerning innovation, Homer's experiences contribute to the expanding documentation of the crucial role modern communications media played (and still play) in the continually changing folk-song scene. Homer states:

My family bought a battery-powered radio—we didn't have electricity in those days—and I started listening to station WSM and the Grand Old Opry; that influenced me a lot because it was the only well-played music I could hear on a regular basis. . . . Of course, I shouldn't leave out the influence of the old spring-wound phonograph; every family tried to have one, would even trade to get one, say trade a hog for a phonograph. I listened to music on the wax records;[6] I remember that I especially enjoyed Buell Kazee's recordings of banjo picking in the real old style.[7] That kind of outside entertainment was all we had; if we had not had the phonograph and later the radio, and traveling entertainers once in a while, then no one except local boys provided entertainment. . . . I suppose the reason I play the type of music that I do even today stems from those early exposures.

The "type of music" Homer plays today is highly varied; it ranges from international traditional ballads to popular and semiclassical works, to "hillbilly" tunes, to original compositions (his own or others)—and of course religious music is always included. However, the preponderance of his repertoire falls into the hillbilly class—or what has popularly come to be called either bluegrass or country-western;[8] Homer's term for this style of music is simply "traditional mountain music," as it was the dominant style that permeated his early musical milieu.

Folk song scholar D.K. Wilgus claims that the year 1927 witnessed what he calls "the great hillbilly watershed . . . which marks a change in hillbilly tradition" as a result of the sudden availability of folk artists' performances on records, which the folk themselves bought and played in vast numbers. It is interesting to note that Homer Ledford was born just at Wilgus's turning point. Wilgus states that until that time "folk performers had been influencing each other, with and without the media of radio and recordings, which of course accelerated the process."[9] The research of Archie Green, also a folksong scholar, likewise affirms the influence of mass media on, and outlines their inter-relationships with, folk songs and folk performers.[10] Wilgus notes of Green's work: "He shows for the first time not only that commercial records can be used to document an oral tradition, but that they may be an integral part of that tradition."[11] Of the influence of recordings in particular, Green states:

> For a people still close to oral tradition, the phonograph was an instrument of compelling importance: relatively inexpensive, easy to play, natural as a source for songs, stories, and instrumental styles. . . . It is not surprising that of all modern technology's aural or visual gifts in this century the sound recording was the easiest assimilated into folk culture. . . . Like some folklorists, I have long accepted the notion that individual recorded songs entered tradition and became 'folksongs' in much the same manner as did broadsides.[12]

Homer Ledford's early musical environment appears to support Green's insights, for popular culture's innovative mass media certainly influenced the development of Homer's musical style, just as other innovative influences on the mountain culture later affected his development as a craftsman. There have always been in Homer's life—whether in person, on records, or on radio—numerous musicians, both perfunctory performers and truly star performers; there were fewer players of dulcimers, however, than of other stringed instruments. In fact, Homer did not see a dulcimer (except in pictures), much less hear one, until he left home at age 18 to attend the John C. Campbell Folk School.

Today, Homer's performing abilities are almost equally demonstrated with several instruments: he plays dulcimer, guitar, recorder, banjo, mandolin, autoharp, ukulele, fiddle, harmonica, jew's harp, and the musical saw;[13] and with any instrument he plays, there is no doubt that Homer is a "star performer" of instrumental folk music. His versatile virtuosity can be appreciated all the more when one realizes that he has never received a formal music lesson in his life. The only two instances of what could conceivably be called musical instruction occurred when Homer was a small boy. One— when he was seven or eight years old—consisted of a week-long series of evening drills in shape note reading and singing, conducted for the public in the community's one-room schoolhouse by one of Homer's uncles. (Homer still has several shape note songbooks;[14] the hymn "New Britain," or "Amazing Grace,"[15] which he learned in the shape note manner, is perhaps one of the more frequently performed items in his repertoire.)

Two or three years later, when Homer was about 10 years old, he received his other bit of "training"—and his first opportunity to learn to play a musical instrument—from his uncle Otis McDonald. Through a mail-order catalog, Homer's uncle had obtained a guitar and an instruction booklet, and he had learned to strum the first five chords; however, after those first chords Mr. McDonald's progress stopped, and he never learned to play. The young Homer pestered his uncle, attempting to borrow the guitar in order to teach himself to play; his uncle finally acquiesced and, before allowing Homer to practice on his own, taught the boy the same five chords he himself had learned earlier. Homer then proceeded to experiment with the guitar and eventually taught himself to play; significantly, however, he did not utilize his uncle's instruction booklet.

As Homer's mastery of the guitar occurred prior to the Ledfords' purchase of a radio or phonograph, Homer imitated the playing of either local or itinerant musicians; therefore, Homer's overall playing development was built upon the foundation of his earlier (and still existing) exposure to personal vis-a-vis performances in his own neighborhood—such as those of the woman who owned the Stella guitar—during which he had the benefit of visual as well as aural learning situations. Later, Homer imitated performances he heard on radio and recordings, and experimented with his own renditions; eventually he learned to play other instruments as well. Because he personally owned no musical instrument (the guitar was, after all, borrowed), Homer, at age 12, decided to remedy the situation by constructing his own instrument—an attempt that was, of course, representative of the inventiveness, self-sufficiency, and craftsmanship of many Appalachian mountaineers.

So ample and recognized is the documentation on this topic that

little needs to be said about the southern Highlander's extreme individuality and his concomitant self-reliance. Perhaps John C. Campbell's succinct remarks are typical: "The Highlander learned by hard
necessity to rely upon himself. . . . The temper of the Highlander is
in fact the independent democratic temper of the frontiersman."[16]
Such was the prevailing attitude on the frontier; however, additional
research needs to be conducted in order to evaluate adequately the
contemporary manifestations of that pioneerlike approach. In frontier days, of course, there was hardly any alternative to every family's providing its own necessities of life; in modern times, either
economic hardship or a basic preference to be self-reliant—or a combination of both—seems to perpetuate the life-style of the pioneer
for many people. The tendency to be a self-reliant home craftsman,
handyman, jack-of-all trades—or what I have termed a "Saturday (or
midnight) mechanic"—seems ubiquitous in American society,
perhaps being most common in small towns and rural areas; it appears to be strongest among those who can trace in either their lineage
or life experience a tradition of such living patterns. The entire do-it-
yourself movement of recent years is very likely a commercial expression of this basic folk motivation and pattern of behavior.

    Growing up in a traditionally self-reliant environment, Homer
displayed an early penchant for carving and generally making things
with his hands, especially from wood; however, as a young boy, he
was without his own pocketknife—as well as his own musical
instrument—until age 12. When he finally did acquire a knife, Homer
made toys for himself and a few small items for his mother, but music
was in the boy's soul. Homer recalls:

> I always loved music and loved to carve and to make things
> with my hands, and I seemed to be pretty good at it; so when
> I got my first pocketknife, for Christmas at age 12, I tried to
> make a musical instrument. I guess that's when it all really
> began. . . . to this day I'm lost without a pocketknife; I always
> carry one with me. . . . The pocketknife is a tremendous tool,
> but of course you have to learn to use it, and that takes a lot
> of time; it's all I had at the start.

With his pocketknife as his only tool, twelve-year-old Homer gathered
whatever scraps of wood and other likely objects he could find—birch
bark, lard cans, dynamite boxes, and pine from a barn—and, using
strands of screen wire for strings, he tried again and again to make
either a banjo or a guitar. He states, "They weren't very successful,

but I just seemed to have to try to make a musical instrument." Even though none of those first endeavors proved very rewarding, they did stimulate Homer's ambition to construct an instrument that could actually be played. When Homer was about 15, that ambition was finally realized. As Homer tells the story:

I visited my uncle [the same uncle whose guitar Homer borrowed—Otis McDonald]; I went with him one time when he was courting a lady who lived about 30 miles away and whose entire family was very musical. It happened that the father of this family was very much of a craftsman. He was not trained, and he didn't make anything for sale, as he didn't know there was any place he could sell anything he made; he made things simply because he wanted to, and he had the spare time. Well, he had made every one of his children a fiddle, using dynamite boxes and just any wood he could find; surprisingly, they all sounded good. One of those fiddles he considered a prize, and he kept it for himself, and every bit of it except the pegs and bridge was made from matchsticks! Now you talk about something hitting me hard, that did; I was stunned, and it proved to be a great inspiration to me. I went back home determined to make an instrument that would be at least almost as good; so I attempted to make a fiddle out of matchsticks too. . . . I couldn't get the top and back to work with matchsticks, so I made the top and back from dynamite boxes; but the sides were made by setting matchsticks side by side on end and gluing them together to join the top and the back. I carved the neck out of a piece of maple which I chopped out of my dad's old maple tree. Well, that fiddle played. But pretty soon if just fell apart; I used the wrong kind of glue, and that summer when the weather got to be humid, the glue wouldn't hold, and the whole fiddle just fell apart; I eventually threw it away.

About one year after the collapse of his matchstick fiddle, Homer tried again, this time not with matchsticks but entirely with maple from his dad's tree except for a hemlock top. With this fiddle, Homer states, "I did a much better job, and I still have it and even play it occasionally. . . . I copied it from pictures in a Montgomery Ward catalog; that was all I had to use for a model. It's no Stradivarius, but it does play, and it stays glued together; from my first one I learned to use waterproof glue. My uncle showed me how to mix varnish and put a finish on it, but that finish doesn't look very good now."

Having succeeded with this fiddle, Homer did not attempt to construct another complete musical instrument until he became familiar with the dulcimer more than two years later. During the interim, he continued, as he says, "to carve on everything in sight" and became so adept with his pocketknife that he was generally recognized in his community as a wood-carver of some merit. Then in 1946, after Homer had been severely ill with rheumatic fever, he was sent as part of his recuperation to the John C. Campbell Folk School in Brasstown, North Carolina; Homer was 18 years old at the time, and that three-month visit proved to be a significant factor in his development as a craftsman of traditional musical instruments.

At the John C. Campbell Folk School, Homer met people who influenced him to cultivate further his penchants for the carving of mountain craft objects and woodworking in general, and for folk music. Of course, the school regularly provided instruction in these areas as part of its curriculum, but to the young Homer Ledford it seemed that such things should be learned naturally, as part of one's environmental heritage, rather than through formalized education. He was not recalcitrant, however—quite the contrary: Homer eagerly utilized his time at the school to learn, in a somewhat academic fashion, more about the activities with which he was already familiar. As Homer recalls, "They introduced me, in a large way, to things I was already very interested in but didn't know much about; for example, I liked folk music, but I didn't know much about it—certainly not in a scholarly vein."

In general, his John C. Campbell Folk School period could no doubt be understood as something of a revitalization, yet Homer's recollections of his experiences there do not even suggest that he personally was "revitalized." Rather, the people at the school esteemed Homer and his talents and merely encouraged him to continue what he was already doing; they also used Homer as an example of what Appalachians could achieve. After all, the original purpose of the school was "to help young people take advantage of their natural powers and to make their life in the country better, more efficient and more interesting."[17]

Homer has very fond memories of Mrs. Campbell, who gave him her own fiddle after asking him to repair it for her; he still has it. Homer recalls, "She said, 'I'm just going to give it to you; just take care of it, and play it.' She knew I played some. Now, I wouldn't let that fiddle go for anything. It's a good old German fiddle. . . . it's over a hundred years old, been in their family a long time." Homer feels that Mrs. Campbell had already planned to give him the fiddle when she asked him to repair it. She knew that he fiddled some for dancing and was part of a small group that played music for the people at the school. He suspects that Mrs. Campbell wanted to see whether he repaired the fiddle properly, and to hear him play it, before she presented it to him. At that time, Mrs. Campbell was about 80 years old, Homer believes, and in good health, though Mr. Campbell had been dead for some time.[18] Homer says of her:

> She was a dear lady; she was my favorite, really. Now some there, I always had the feeling that they were looking down at all of us. Mrs. Campbell wasn't that way; she didn't mind if you didn't have anything; if you had a lot it didn't matter; you were a person to her, really a person, and she was down there with you if you were down there. Some would laugh with you and later laugh at you; they think they're fooling you but they're not. Many people took a lot of us for fools, you know, but if you've got any sense at all—after a while, at least—you can figure it out. . . . If preachers or missionaries wouldn't come and spend the night with you, wouldn't eat with you, wouldn't sit down at the same old table that you did—forget them.

Mrs. Campbell's philosophy is perhaps best stated in her own words: "As Carlyle said of the clay on the potter's wheel, it cannot be formed without being first set in motion, so education cannot be forced on the stagnant mind. The longing for education springs from the feeling of hope, a trust in the future inspired by a prospect of economic emancipation."[19] This is precisely what she provided, though indirectly, for Homer.

During Homer's stay at the school, he saw a dulcimer for the first time: "There were two hanging on the wall behind the piano; one was made by John Jacob Niles while he was there working a great deal with music, and the other one was made by Park Fisher, who used to be in charge of the craft program at the school." Also, one of the officials at the school owned an older dulcimer that had been made by the highly respected traditional Appalachian dulcimer maker J.E. Thomas. Prior to this, Homer had never really comprehended the instrument's musical potential:

> Before I started making [dulcimers], I'd seen pictures of them at home [in family photographs], and then I saw those over

there at Brasstown at the John C. Campbell Folk School hanging on the wall, but at that time I really didn't think too much
of them. They weren't made very pretty, and they didn't have
much finish on them; they were just painted or something.
I didn't think much of them, not only in looks but also
because I found out they were only noted on one string, which
didn't excite me, since I was already playing guitar. I needed
to be educated along that line, and that was what happened;
I met Edna there, and I eventually came to see that this was
really a nice little instrument after all, and I really enjoyed
the sound of it.

"Edna" was Edna Ritchie, who had grown up in a celebrated
dulcimer-playing family in Viper, Kentucky, and was at the school
working as a receptionist.[20] Homer fondly remembers that "she
knew how to play the dulcimer and how to sing, using it as accompaniment . . . so with all of this influence, here I was." Homer credits
Edna with providing several of the tunes in his dulcimer repertoire,
and for teaching him the rudiments of playing the instrument. Edna
herself says that Homer is too generous in his remarks about her contributions to his dulcimer abilities: "All I did was to show him how
to tune it and hold it and where the first note was, and—you know
how good he is—he just started playing it; I did play him some of
my old dulcimer tunes though." Of course, by that time Homer was
already an accomplished self-taught musician, so he quickly became
adept with this small, sweet-sounding instrument. Moreover, the fact
that dulcimers are handcrafted appealed immensely to Homer Ledford, the carver and woodworker.

Homer's youthful proclivity for crafting musical instruments
received perhaps its greatest impetus when one of the officials at the
school asked him to repair a damaged dulcimer: "Marguerite Butler
Bidstrup one day brought me a dulcimer she had that someone in the
mountains had given them;[21] one of the sides had come out of it,
and she wanted me to repair it. This is really where I gained some
knowledge of the construction of the instrument. I became real interested in it; when I took it apart and repaired it and glued it back
together, it sort of became a part of me." Homer's repair work was
highly praised, and subsequently he was asked to make minor repairs
on another dulcimer, which belonged to someone who was attending
the school. School officials were so impressed with Homer's work
that when they received inquiries from Southern Highlanders, Inc.
(a craft shop on Fifth Avenue in New York City), they approached

Homer about constructing entire dulcimers: "It seems that [the shop] was searching for someone to make two dulcimers, to fill two orders they had received. . . . Well, the school asked me if I would make these two for the craft shop in New York, and I did."

With some amusement, Homer recalls how those two dulcimers led to further orders:

> I couldn't figure out how to mail them, so I hung around the school for two weeks trying to figure out how. As it turned out, it was lucky that I did, because two groups of people came to the school for short courses in recreation—there was one in June and one in July—and about 40 people came each time, from all over. Well, when they saw those two dulcimers I made, they just went wild, and I got eight more orders but had to go back to Tennessee to make them. You know, I only charged twenty dollars apiece, which was about what it cost to make them—but boy, that was a lot of money to a poor mountain boy then.
>
> Anyway, that started it all; those people advertised to others, and I have been getting orders ever since. . . . I guess you could say it was accidental, but even if that had not happened, I still would have been making musical instruments, but no doubt I wouldn't have had the market for my work that developed because of the connections at the school. Then too, I seem to have been one of only two people in the southern mountains who at that time made dulcimers, at least for sale; no one else was making them in other than local or private situations, or so the people at the school said, anyway. . . . The other one they said was Jethro Amburgey at Hindman, Kentucky[22] . . . but there are lots of dulcimer makers now.

One of the very early Ledford dulcimers was acquired by Edna Ritchie, who still owns it (fig. 1). At the time, Homer did not realize that his ability held real potential for monetary profit; his dulcimer making began, he says, as a hobby, "just something I wanted to do." Though referring to the dulcimer market in general, music scholar Charles Seeger's comments can serve to summarize Homer's situation: "Owing partly to the encouragement of rural handicrafts by urban trained social workers during the last fifty years, and partly to the nationwide folk music revival movement in the cities since 1940, a number of makers have found a market among urban amateurs. I

1. Edna Ritchie Baker with early Ledford dulcimer

have, however, never known of a factory made instrument. . . . Its making and its use have taken place within the currency of an oral tradition of music."[23] Homer himself was to perpetuate that tradition.

After his three-month stay at the John C. Campbell Folk School, Homer returned home, where he made and shipped the eight dulcimers ordered at the school. Naturally, he related his school experiences to his family and was delighted to hear, in turn, his grandmother relate her youthful memories of dulcimers: "She told me stories about people who used to have them and play them; she knew a lot about them; several of her stories dealt with two troubadors who had dulcimers and who used to travel through our area playing for their keep, but none of *my* family ever owned any instruments other than guitars. . . . except for a mandolin one of my brothers bought."

Seemingly, Homer felt that dulcimers were instruments of the past, belonging to the era of his grandmother's youth and earlier. No doubt the guitar, mandolin, banjo, and fiddle had slowly supplanted the dulcimer among most Appalachian families. Then too, radio and recording artists of that time rarely performed on the dulcimer. As a result, in Homer's youth the dulcimer usually was to be found only in folk schools, museums, and the like, or occasionally in the possession of a family—such as the Ritchies—who tenaciously cherished the little instrument. Maud Karpele's statement typifies the situation: "The dulcimer . . . we saw and heard in some of the Kentucky mountain schools and never in the homes of the people, where it is evidently but rarely to be found."[24] There seems to be some support for the claim that the dulcimer was principally of Kentucky provenance; if true, this would help to explain its near-disappearance outside Kentucky, certainly by the time Homer came along. John C. Campbell noted that the dulcimer "is rare, and with one exception the writer has never met it outside the mountains of Kentucky."[25] Thanks to Homer and others, however, the dulcimer is now well represented not only in Appalachian homes but elsewhere throughout the United States and, indeed, even the world.

Homer continued making dulcimers one by one as he received orders for them, but at that point he never considered relying solely upon his craft for a livelihood. So in 1949 he entered Berea College in Berea, Kentucky, under a Vocational Rehabilitation grant, hoping one day to become an industrial arts teacher, and thereby share with others his natural talent and love of working with wood to create fine things.

While attending Berea, Homer utilized his skill as a carver to earn

2. Some of Homer's carvings

his way.[26] Examples of the types of wood carving he produced at this stage in the development of his craft may be seen on figure 2 (such items are now strictly auxiliary to his musical instruments). While at Berea, Homer of course acquired academic knowledge about folk music, and both academic and practical knowledge about woodworking; moreover, he met other people there who had parallel interests and who consequently influenced and inspired him to nurture his interests in folk music and musical instruments. It was also at Berea that Homer met his future wife, Colista, who has since supported and encouraged him in his development as a musical instrument craftsman. Colista also plays the dulcimer and the guitar, and sings.[27] One of the finest dulcimers Homer has ever made was an anniversary present for Colista (the sketch on page 24 is based on this instrument). During his years at Berea, Homer continued to make dulcimers on a per-order basis, and occasionally he would make other instruments as well.

Unfortunately, Berea did not have an industrial arts program that would provide teaching credentials. Consequently, as he was determined to enroll in a fully accredited industrial arts program, Homer left Berea in 1952 and matriculated at what was then called Eastern Kentucky State Teachers College, at Richmond;[28] he graduated in 1954 with a B.S. degree in industrial arts. After graduation, Homer immediately moved to Louisville, Kentucky, and taught industrial arts for one year in the public school system there. When the school year ended, Homer returned to Berea for a summer job demonstrating techniques of carving before curtain time and during intermissions of the Wilderness Road summer drama, which played (and still plays) annually at the Indian Fort Theatre just outside the town. That summer (1955) Homer was informed of an opening for a teacher of industrial arts in the Clark County School System at Winchester, Kentucky, 40 miles from Berea. Homer obtained that position and held it, teaching industrial arts full time and making dulcimers and other instruments in his spare time, until 1963, when he resigned in order to devote all of his time to dulcimer making.

Since 1963, Homer's social and family life has more and more revolved around his craft, music, and related activities. For example, he has contributed significantly to the establishment and expansion of the Kentucky Guild of Artists and Craftsmen: he is a charter member, has served two terms on its board of directors, and regularly participates in the guild's fairs (held twice annually—May and October—at Indian Fort Theatre in Berea). In addition, Homer is frequently invited to attend other fairs and festivals, ranging from those sponsored by the National Endowment for the Arts and other governmental agencies to local grass-roots endeavors like the annual Festival of the Bluegrass in Lexington, Kentucky. Homer regularly attends five such annual events, where he displays and sells his instruments, discusses his work with other craftsmen and curious passersby, and at times performs. Often his family accompanies him and sometimes performs with him. A special honor was bestowed upon Homer when, during the annual dulcimer convention at Pine Mountain State Park, in September of 1978, the Kentucky State Department of Parks designated the affair a "Homer Ledford Weekend"; Homer was recognized and honored for his invaluable contributions to traditional dulcimer craftsmanship, and he was also applauded for his expertise as a traditional mountain musician. He responded by presenting three concerts.

In addition to craft fairs and festivals, Homer is regularly invited

THE LEDFORD THREE-STRING DULCIMER

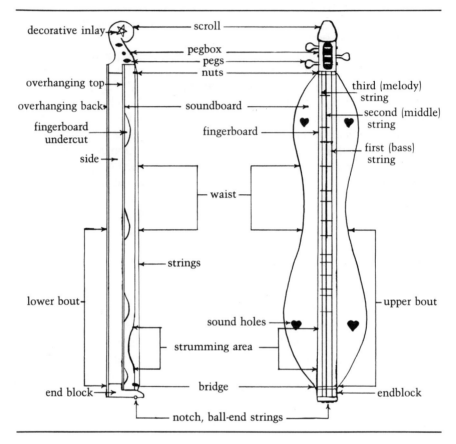

decorative inlay — scroll
pegbox
pegs
nuts

overhanging top
third (melody) string
overhanging back — soundboard
second (middle) string
fingerboard undercut — fingerboard
first (bass) string
side

waist

strings

lower bout
upper bout

sound holes
strumming area

end block
bridge
endblock
notch, ball-end strings

to participate in workshops and seminars sponsored by various civic groups and academic institutions. He has taught and demonstrated both folk music and folk instrument craftsmanship at Eastern Kentucky University and at a National Wildlife Federation-sponsored workshop at Black Mountain, North Carolina, and he has shared his knowledge with faculty and students of the Appalachian Studies program at the University of Kentucky. Homer is also the subject of a videotape prepared by Eastern Kentucky University for National Educational Television.

In Winchester, Kentucky, where Homer has lived since 1955, he is often called upon to perform by various institutions and organizations. He plays annually for the Lion's Club, at several area elementary and secondary schools, and at Winchester's grass-roots fair; he also takes his music to the local nursing home.

Homer and Colista are also active in a group called the Lexington Folksingers. Although the group's membership numbers only about 25, actual attendance is usually higher since these members regularly invite friends, relatives, and acquaintances to the monthly get-togethers. Participants come from various occupational, social, and educational levels, and the age span encompasses both an 11-year old fiddler and such relative old-timers as Edna Ritchie Baker (and—until their deaths—the well-known banjo picker and singer Buell Kazee, and Edna's husband, Floyd). The common denominator for the group is, of course, their interest in folk music. At the meetings, held each month at a different member's home, each participant performs— with instrument or voice or both—whatever numbers he or she desires. The repertoire of the group includes a smattering of all types of music, the preponderance being, of course, some form of folk music; occasionally, however, someone will perform a song of his or her own creation, and some of these originals have gained group acceptance, thus creating a very esoteric sort of folk music within the group. Everyone is encouraged to perform, from the youngest to the oldest. There is group singing for those who hesitate to perform solo, and given the wide assortment of instruments present—usually guitar, banjo, fiddle, mandolin, recorder, harmonica, autoharp, and dul- cimer—there are numerous ensemble instrumental performances, as well.

Homer has organized a group picturesquely named "Homer Led- ford and the Cabin Creek Band" (after a creek in the county where Homer lives), consisting of five members who perform mainly bluegrass music on a typical array of instruments: guitar, fiddle, bass, banjo, harmonica, mandolin, dulcimer, saw, and autoharp. Homer, of course, plays all of these instruments, but in the band he most often plays the mandolin, which he considers the most difficult stringed instrument of its type to master (I have heard many other traditional musicians corroborate Homer's assertion). The band appears at various area festivals and fairs, performs for private parties, and played three times for John Lair at the world-renowned Renfro Valley Barn Dance. Reportedly, Mr. Lair liked the group so much that he endeavored to get them to play at Renfro Valley on a regular basis; and since Lair is viewed by anyone knowledgeable about traditional music, and its modern performance, as one of its more astute ap- praisers, the invitation indeed constituted high praise.

Homer's instrumental repertoire—how he learned and developed the tunes, and under what influences—will be dealt with in a separate study, but it is noteworthy here that Homer seems able to learn nearly any piece of music and, if he cares to, perform it quite skillfully. His instrumental repertoire has been influenced by church music, the Ritchie family (especially Edna), experiences at the John C. Campbell Folk School and Berea College, Billy Edd Wheeler, and generally all people he has come into contact with who share his background; in other words, his repertoire (and Homer himself confirms this) reflects the personalities of those who share similar traditions with him and with each other. Homer only rarely dissociates his music from its makers, and he nearly always gives credit to the creator of the music he plays, even to anonymous "folk." Only with religious music does Homer fail to associate his tunes with a personality; rather, he attributes them to a group sharing similar religious, socioeconomic, and cultural traditions.

Neither in his solo playing nor in the band does Homer sing with his instrumental music. As a matter of fact, I have never heard Homer sing in performance. He sings regularly only during religious services, when all present also sing, and then in such an indistinguishable manner that one can scarcely see his lips move. He confesses that once many years ago, during an informal round-robin, he was enticed to sing, but the reaction was such that he vowed never again to undertake a vocal performance. Indeed, his oral performance abilities, he is quick to agree, are rather limited; he is not even much of a storyteller, although his uncle Otis McDonald—who had so marked an influence on him—is an accomplished raconteur. Homer has apparently always deferred to his uncle in this respect, which perhaps partially accounts for Homer's storytelling reticence to this day. He is an excellent conversationalist, however; in fact, it is often difficult for an interviewer to control the dialogue, as once Homer starts talking, tangential and parenthetical information and discussion flow freely. Homer's loquacity is a fact of his maturity; as a youth he was withdrawn and taciturn. Today, Homer is fond of interlarding his discourse with brief quasi-memorates (the folklorist's term for personal experience stories); for lack of a better expression, I call these "I-oriented anecdotes." They represent Homer's nearest approach to folkloric narrative.

The postulations of linguist Dell Hymes concerning four main categories of communicative competence are pertinent[29] to an appreciation of Homer's musical abilities. Hymes distinguishes his somewhat evolutionary categories by analyzing a performer's ability to (1) interpret, (2) report, (3) repeat, (4) perform. The fourth category, performance, Hymes believes involves true creativity; category three, repetition, although demanding thorough expertise in effective communication techniques, usually requires only more or less perfunctory execution. Many folkloric events reflect category-three characteristics, while perhaps those events presented by persons often referred to by folklorists as "star performers" are the events most often manifesting aspects of truly memorable, often creative, performance—Hymes's category four. It is in this category that the majority of Homer's instrumental endeavors would be listed; he nearly always "performs" when he plays. The only recurring instances I can detect when he plays *without* "performing" seem to be (1) when he tunes and tries out a newly constructed or newly repaired instrument for the first time, and (2) when he is in the company of only a very few, well-known people (or thinks he is alone) and is playing randomly for relaxation, or perhaps experimenting—either with music or with the instrument itself. Yet I have been present when even in these situations Homer's playing could aptly be rated near performance level.

Homer's expertise is such that he often includes, as part of a formal performance, several vaudeville-style "tricks;" for example, he uses the traditional Appalachian wooden dolls that dance on the end of a string attached to his fingers while he plays the banjo. In recent years, as the frequency of his appearances has increased, these comic segments have come to constitute a larger place in his total presentation. As Homer says, every performer knows several different ways to perform, and when a folk or mountain musician begins to rely upon performance for his livelihood, he invariably interjects various frills into his presentations. For example, Homer recalls from his childhood a folk musician who traveled through the mountains and made his living by playing his banjo and dancing his wooden doll; "he was hoping everybody would keep him a night or two or a week, or whatever, and feed him, and he would entertain."

Yet novelties such as the dancing doll, Homer contends, although traditional in the mountains, were usually demonstrated only for close friends or family members; and vaudeville activities actually constitute only a minor portion of a Ledford appearance. Perhaps typical was Homer's performance in 1971 when he won the folk instrumental music division of the Tri-State Folk Festival. He played only two dulcimers for that event, which was the first such contest in which he ever competed; his performance repertoire, reflecting the typical array of dulcimer tunes in his general repertoire, included "Old Joe Clarke," "Goodbye Liza Jane," "Wildwood Flower," "Pretty Pol-

3. Homer's traditional performing stance

ly," "New Britain" ("Amazing Grace"). These were all done in a traditional manner; indeed, I have never seen Homer perform with the dulcimer in other than his very traditional style. He is adamant in his insistence that dulcimer playing should remain strictly traditional; he cites with much distaste another performer's effort to electrify a dulcimer being played in competition.

Comments made by Homer during the 1971 contest provide an idea of his style: "The dulcimer hasn't the chromatic scale of the guitar . . . so when a tune demands a half-step, such as 'Old Joe Clarke,' I push the string over onto the fret to simulate a chromatic half-step; this produces a 'whang' sound, but in tune context it does provide the needed note. . . . Usually on fast tunes I add the typical mountain ending, 'shave and a haircut—two-bits,' and often I add the whangy half-step to it, as well. On slower tunes, especially 'New Britain,' I like to use the vibrato effect."

Of course, the two dulcimers—one three-string and one four-string—that Homer played in the contest were his own creations; he only rarely performs with instruments he himself has not handcrafted. It is with the dulcimer that Homer's playing style perhaps seems least individualistic. In fact, it seems very similar to the traditional style described by Charles Seeger[30] except that Homer seldom uses a "noter" to hold the melody string against the frets, preferring the better control afforded by his fingers. Nor does he use a quill, but most often a felt pick; the quill seems affected to him, and unlike his more flamboyant performances with other musical instruments, his dulcimer playing is always very intent and serious, his posture almost reverent (fig. 3). With other instruments he often consciously and purposely imitates someone else's style (always giving credit to the imitated artist), such as that of Bill Monroe, Earl Scruggs, Buell Kazee, Billy Edd Wheeler, or the Carter family. When Homer plays in his own excellent style, he still no doubt partially reflects the styles of less prominent performers in his background—for instance, Bob Collins the traveling fiddler, or other musicians from his youthful environment—most of whom, Homer believes and is quick to state, were not of the same caliber as the "stars" he heard on the radio or on records.

In addition to being a self-taught musician, Homer is, in the familiar folkloric pattern, essentially a self-taught craftsman. His explanation of his youthful persistence is simply that "I just seemed to have to try to make a musical instrument."[31] However, when he was questioned more closely regarding his early motivation, his poignant response was as follows:

Ever since I can remember, I just always wanted to do things, but if I analyze it a little bit, going back to when I was real young, we had become a put-down bunch because we didn't have anything. . . . Sometimes we'd go into town and we'd see people who had things, and we were constantly wanting those things also, but like they say, no way to buy it. I always somehow had it in the back of my mind that I was going to change all that . . . and the only way I could change all that was to do it myself with my own hands. And again I remember sitting out on that old woodpile more than once—it would nearly all be red cedar, *beautiful* red cedar Dad cut up, or I would, to burn in the cookstove; it burned good and of course it whittled good. So I sat there and whittled, and I wanted to be a great carver. I'd think about those school books and I'd remember a carver we read about in a story in one of the books; I never thought, I guess, that I really would, but I was dreaming anyway.

I had some sort of ambition, and so I got to going back over to the old high school building. This is part of the story: the old high school closed when I was a junior; after my junior year I had to go into Livingston to a consolidated school. They closed that old church school 'cause there weren't but 45 students and four teachers, and the state wouldn't let it exist like that; so anyway, when they closed it they still had that old shop there. . . . And I would go back over there because the people that run the grounds and everything were really good friends of our family. They'd let me use that shop by myself—just go out there and get the keys and use that shop by myself, all the fine equipment there and everything—tools, you know. There was a carpenter around there who did all the carpenter work, and he was a *fine* carpenter. I learned a lot from him because he was so good at it, and he would show me, he didn't mind showing me. . . . I got a lot of kind of practical experience—just blundering through it except for what he showed me, and he was a carpenter and didn't know that much about finish work. But I would make little things—I'd turn a bowl or use the lathe, you know, because it fascinated me so much.

My uncle lived right across the pasture field from us, and he was a carpenter and also a blacksmith, and he began to show me some stuff when he saw I was interested. He even let me borrow his handsaw; he never loaned anybody his handsaw. And so it went, just one of those things that I just had to be doing it because there was no one else to do it; you couldn't buy it. And it had to be musical instruments eventually because I loved music so dearly; I loved it; it wouldn't matter what was playing, it seemed like I liked it.

Well, we never listened to classical music 'cause there wasn't any classical music; not even on the radio . . . it was all country music. And so that's all I knew and that's what I wanted, and of course not being able to buy musical instruments, my biggest aim was . . . to make a fiddle and a guitar out of birch bark. Then I made the first fiddle that played out of maple cut out of dad's old maple tree and some hemlock, which I thought was spruce.

It's just that childhood thing, you know, if you don't have it and you want it so badly, and I did. I did feel that I had a knack for things, you know, that I could make things with my hands or just an old knife from the table. I took a file and sharpened one of Mother's old table knives. . . . I whittled with it until Mother finally got me a knife for a Christmas present, and that was my first pocketknife.

To this day Homer continues to use one of his mother's knives; he has removed the handle and filed the blade so that it can function as a scraper, usually to remove excess glue from glued joints. Homer says that he has kept his mother's knife because it contains superior steel, but it is apparent that he also keeps it to remind him of his beginnings, both as a boy in his mother's care and as a neophyte Appalachian carver and craftsman.

So, as a child whittling with first a file-sharpened table knife and then a pocketknife, Homer started making some of the things he wanted. He made several toys, and he gradually perfected his original talent by becoming expert with the basic hand tools of his craft; he has also incorporated into his work a few modern power tools, the use of which he learned chiefly in college. Still, Homer's expertise in handcrafting musical instruments has derived from essentially nonacademic, informal sources and exposures, though the two schools he attended did extend his experience with woodworking in general. Berea helped him first to realize and then to apply to best advantage the art of a master carver, though he was nearly one before he enrolled; Eastern Kentucky helped him to develop a thorough knowledge of modern woodworking tools and machines.

The modern power tools Homer uses are the basic large job tools found in any home workshop: jointer, band saw, drill press, and table saw. To satisfy his unique needs, however, Homer has broadened their standard functions and has designed completely new and innovative attachments for some of them; for example, he has made special cutting heads for his saws so they will rip woods to the proper thickness and in the fine manner needed specifically for the dulcimer. Moreover, even his modern hand tools exhibit many nonstandard features. He has altered several conventional items to satisfy the specific requirements of his craft; others are entirely of his own design. Homer continually emphasizes that it has taken many years to achieve the degree of excellence now reflected in all of his work, and his slow and deliberate development and refinement of the tools of his craft have in no small way contributed to that end:

> At first I had no idea of construction standards except by looking at mail-order catalogs . . . Of course, the dulcimers I examined and repaired at the John C. Campbell Folk School gave me intricate knowledge about the instrument's construction. Some neighborhood boys did have guitars, but I was more interested in experimenting with my own work than copying one exactly as it was; of course, I didn't have available to me either proper tools or the correct types of woods needed for musical instruments, so the quality of my work, compared with conventional standards . . . was slow in becoming perfected. From the time I made my first instrument until about 1950 . . . my work was not of the high quality that it is now; since 1950 I feel that all of my instruments have been something I can really take pride in having made.

In 1950 Homer constructed what he considers to be his "first exceptionally fine instrument": a mandolin. He still has it (fig. 4); it plays well and has maintained its attractiveness. To provide himself with basic ideas and a model, Homer examined a closeup photograph of a mandolin used by Bill Monroe and his Bluegrass Boys; in addition, he experienced the feel—the balance, weight, proportions, and so on—of the instrument by examining and playing a mandolin he had purchased through a mail-order house. Of all the instruments he makes, Homer considers the mandolin to be the most challenging; in the time required to create one mandolin, he could construct several dulcimers. Yet his mandolins certainly warrant the time required to produce them; for example, Bill Monroe once tried out the Ledford mandolin discussed above and commented that it was perhaps

4. Homer's first mandolin and recent fancy mandolin

the finest he had ever played; Homer highly appreciated this compliment from such a virtuoso as Bill Monroe. Homer has made instruments for several folk performers, among them Billy Edd Wheeler, whom he has known since they were both students at Berea College.[32]

This sort of quality is achieved only through true dedication, long experience, and hard work. As Homer explains:

I am always amused when people come here and want to learn how to make a dulcimer in, say one week. Some even come with their own homemade dulcimers, put together perhaps over a month's time, and they say they have thought of quitting their jobs to make dulcimers full time. It's a mistake; they can't produce quality dulcimers overnight. . . . When I quit teaching to make instruments full time . . . I had already been making dulcimers for 17 years; then too, I gave guitar and banjo lessons and also made guitars and banjos, and I was carving wooden jewelry. Now, of course, I have dropped music lessons entirely, most of the other carving, and nearly all banjo and guitar orders, and devote [nearly] full time to my dulcimers.

In contrast to Homer's views, one folkcraft revival proponent suggests that constructing a quality dulcimer is "something that anyone should be able to do."[33] Such statements should be taken *cum grano salis* at best. I know of several dulcimer makers—even in Appalachia—who have been constructing these instruments for some while, but whose dulcimers are poor examples of the craft when compared with Homer's. Apparently some dulcimer makers consciously strive to produce an instrument that appears to be roughly constructed, often to an exaggerated degree; perhaps they feel that today's general public, and particularly the tourist buyer of curios and novelties, equates rough or shoddy construction with "folksiness." Homer does not stoop to such misguided efforts to appeal to the public's preconceived notions of what is folksy; as a proud traditional Appalachian craftsman, he simply strives to produce the very best dulcimer he can. Many of the traditional Appalachian dulcimer makers of years past adhered to relatively high standards; moreover, those Appalachians who bought the instruments were able to judge craftsmanship and preferred to buy quality. The best craftsmen—such as Homer—do not purposely produce a rough-appearing product to appeal to the warped notions that the buying public may harbor concerning folk handicrafts.

Homer continues:

Experience, and a lot of it, over several years is what is needed to be able to produce a really fine dulcimer. . . . Right to begin with, if you don't know what sort of woods to use and where to find them properly aged and of adequate dimensions, it's impossible to proceed with any hope of success. And you can read books or look at pictures or even examine several different instruments in detail, but if you don't have years of experience, you won't make a good instrument. Then too, you have to love to make them; every time I make an instrument I feel that a little of me goes into it.

When I'm making a dulcimer, I don't think about the money; I think about the joy I get out of it and so on. It's really something to make all the parts from scratch and then put 'em all together, and then there it is, a beautiful little dulcimer; and people can use it and can learn to play it and enjoy it.[34]

Another dulcimer maker, apparently agreeing with Homer, states that "the primary requirement is a love for the dulcimer."[35]

A pointed illustration of Homer's very personal, and often emotional, identification with his craft occurred one summer Sunday afternoon in the Ledfords' front yard when a prospective customer came by. Several of Homer's instruments were lying around or leaning against chairs; the young girl, who was interested in a dulcimer, nearly stepped on one. Homer cautioned, "Watch out; if you step on one of my instruments, you're a-walking on me." Though spoken in good humor, there was no doubt that Homer's statement accurately reflected his feeling for his handcrafted instruments.

When I asked Homer to explain any possible secret of success beyond his obvious love of and innate talent for musical instrument craftsmanship, he answered:

I don't have a trade secret; if I'm successful, it all boils down to the reason being that it's exactly because I like it; that is what I *had* to do, ever since I can remember; I had to make things by hand. . . . now it's true I've used machinery since I've been able to own some, but I don't use the machine as an assembly line, or even as an automatic worker; I control it for each and every job. . . . you have to be careful not to let the machine entice you into taking the skill out of your work, and use it only for large patterns or block cuts and the like; I still always put the handmade touch to all parts of each instrument. . . . And there is only me; I'm a one-man dulcimer shop.

Being a "one-man shop" consumes nearly all of Homer's daylight hours, usually five but often six days a week the year round. He is kept particularly busy supplying dulcimers for about eight craft shops, as well as filling direct orders. For the craft shops he most often constructs a three-string dulcimer with standard woods, but for personal

5. Homer's banjos

orders he will make either a three- or four-string instrument, and he
will use antique and other special woods. Only rarely can or will he
accept an order for another kind of instrument, so in demand are his
dulcimers. To date Homer has constructed approximately 4,792
dulcimers; 18 ukuleles (he no longer makes these), 375 banjos—both
the fretless "mountain" banjo and a "professional" model (fig. 5); 15
guitars (which he no longer makes, fig. 6); 9 mandolins (fig. 4); and
3 fiddles (he has never constructed a fiddle for sale). He has also made
a few teardrop-shaped dulcimers and double sweetheart dulcimers (fig.
7); these, however, are special-order items. Homer has accurate sales
records for all of his instruments except the first two dulcimers.

6. Homer's guitar

It perhaps seems uncanny, but I have never met anyone who did not like Homer's dulcimers. Each of the numerous customers I questioned expressed more than satisfaction with his instrument; most were proud of their dulcimers, insisted that I see them, and wanted to know whether I owned one. Most also were somewhat puzzled, but pleasantly so, that Homer could manage to produce such a fine instrument for such a relatively reasonable price. Homer has always, as far as I can ascertain, priced his dulcimers below those of most other traditional craftsmen. He mantains that he does not do so intentionally, but rather that he simply tries to keep the price at a figure

that will allow him a reasonable profit; he has stated several times
that he "never hoped to make a lot of money" from his craft but just
a "reasonable living." He has a conscious commitment to produce
an instrument that nearly anyone can afford yet that any customer,
as well as the craftsman himself, can be proud to display. Furthermore, Homer guarantees each of his instruments (although very few
have ever required any repair).

Since the 1950's, Homer has been unable to supply completely
the demand for his dulcimers; the increased demand at that time quite
likely reflected the intensity of the folk music and arts-and-crafts
revival which was then newly sweeping the country.[36] Some
changes in Homer's dulcimers and a concomitant peak in the quality of his craft occurred during the same period. Homer states: "When
I started making [dulcimers] in increased numbers, I made a few
changes in the basic design. . . . I broadened the width of the body
slightly and made the body a little deeper to improve the sound,
broadened the fingerboard some in order to make noting easier, and
redesigned the pegbox to suit my own aesthetic notions. Perhaps some
of these changes, at least in part, account for the increased number
of orders." The changes to which Homer refers include increasing the
width of the dulcimer body, at its widest point, from 6 to 7 inches
and its depth from 1 1/4 to 1 1/2 inches; broadening the fingerboard
from 1 1/8 to 1 3/8 inches; and tapering the pegbox (the overall length
he kept at 34 inches).

Even with these modifications, Homer's design has remained
traditional and perhaps most resembles the well-known J.E. Thomas
dulcimer. Mr. Thomas (1850-1933), of Bath, Kentucky, made well over
1,000 dulcimers in his lifetime, and his instruments have come to
be considered typical of the early traditional Appalachian dulcimer.[37]
Homer now believes, though he did not realize it at the time, that
one dulcimer he repaired at the John C. Campbell Folk School was
either an actual early Thomas or nearly identical to it; because the
instrument was broken, the maker's card—usually placed inside the
dulcimer—had evidently been lost. Though there are several variations, the majority of Appalachian dulcimers are traditionally crafted
with only a very limited number of basic shapes.[38] The Thomas
dulcimer (and Homer's) is perhaps the most widely known and most
prolific type.

The only other early changes in Homer's dulcimers involved the
number of strings and the shape of the sound holes. At first Homer
would construct only three-string dulcimers, but beginning about
1961 he started to make a four-string version as well. He explains:

7. Homer's sweetheart and teardrop dulcimers

The reason I changed was because of so much demand on me
to make a four-string . . . but I didn't want to because I had
this crazy idea that it wasn't a traditional dulcimer. But that
was wrong, I was just hard-headed. . . . From my experience
at the time, I just didn't know that many four-string dulcimers
existed; the more common kind had three strings, and I was
basing my attitude on that. . . . I guess you could say
dulcimers are traditional as long as they have no more than
eight strings. . . . Jean's study[39] brought out more about the
various number of strings, and then I began to talk to some
old people who had owned dulcimers and who knew or had
had dulcimer makers in their family, and I found out that
some actually did [have four strings].

Paradoxically, the southern Highlander's characteristic insistence
upon the rights and vicissitudes of individuality[40] for a long while
prevented Homer from making a dulcimer with the traditional heart-
shaped sound holes. Homer recalls:

When I started making them, in 1946, I wanted to be different.
Now this is something that runs right through the mountains
just as true—just like Jesse Stuart's *The Thread That Runs
So True*;[41] there's a competitive spirit, a *very* competitive
spirit, among craftsmen and musicians in the mountain country, and you want to be different, somehow, from the others—
want to make something different. . . . So did I; I wanted to
be different with the sound hole, so I thought I'd use the diamond instead of the heart, like a playing card pattern. I was
a stickler for that for a long time, too; I wouldn't make a
dulcimer with a heart-shaped sound hole. They kept hammer-
ing away at me though, to make the heart-shaped sound
holes—they really like them, romantic you know—and so
eventually I did. . . . It's funny, too, because I liked it when
I started and have enjoyed making them ever since. . . . From
1946 to about 1965, they had all been diamond-shaped sound
holes; they had a hard time talking me into making anything
else. That was being too much of a stickler, I guess. But
another thing, too: that was my mark; I had it in my mind
that that was my mark, that diamond. I could tell, I thought,
that if I saw a picture of a dulcimer with a diamond-shaped
hole, chances are it was mine; but now I'm lost, and I can
only tell for sure from a distance if a dulcimer is mine from
the taper of the head of the pegbox and the basic shape.

Because the Appalchian dulcimer's traditional shapes have been perpetuated, the production of dulcimers in recent years by various nontraditional, principally urban, makers has brought much copying of the tradition-based designs of established craftsmen such as Homer: "I know I've been copied some, and at first I didn't like it. . . . but I guess I got to thinking about it and thought, well, if they copied it they must have liked it; and copying, I guess, really says something about your work."

One of the more amusing instances of craftsmen copying various aspects of Homer's dulcimer design occurred in relation to the positioning of the double string on his four-string instrument. A double string—two strings placed close together and played as one—is not traditional on the dulcimer; Homer began using it several years ago to facilitate noting and finger movement on the four-string instrument; at that time he positioned the double string in the *middle* of the fingerboard, between the two other strings, so that the player could use the first finger to press it down rather than attempt to hold down two strings with the third finger. Utilizing this design, Homer constructed a teardrop dulcimer for Edna Ritchie Baker, but because Edna's husband, Floyd, who always used a wooden noter rather than his fingers to play the dulcimer, was having difficulty depressing the double string in the middle, Edna asked Homer to position the double string on the *outside*, so that Floyd could more easily get to it with his wooden noter; this Homer did.

At that time the Bakers were performing for many programs; consequently, their tear-drop dulcimer, with the double string on the outside, received rather extensive publicity and was viewed by several newer dulcimer craftsmen, who—believing the placement of the double string to be traditional—promptly copied it. In subsequent years some of these same craftsmen, when they had occasion to see Homer and examine his instruments, asked him why he placed his double string in the middle instead of on the outside "where it belonged" as they believed that was the "traditional" way to do it! Little did they realize that Homer had invented the double-string arrangement and had put it in the middle position and that Floyd and Edna's special dulcimer was the only one, at that time, that Homer had ever made with an outside double string. What the other dulcimer craftsmen had copied and were claiming to be traditional was in fact unique. Furthering the irony, dulcimers mass-produced by Sears, Roebuck and by South Korean and Czechoslovakian companies now also feature the outside double string that originated with the one dulcimer Homer custom-made for the Bakers.

More disturbing than this outstanding example of *mis*copying and erroneous interpretation is the accurate commercial copying of Homer's undercut dulcimer fingerboard, an innovation that one foreign company not only features as a major selling point, but claims to have originated. It must be remembered that Homer's instruments were the first traditional Appalachian dulcimers to be commercially marketed to the general public in any extensive fashion (earlier craftsmen for the most part either sold their dulcimers locally or traded them). Homer was the first traditional dulcimer craftsman to market his dulcimers extensively through commercial outlets in order to sell them to the general public. Homer designed the undercut fingerboard early in the development of his craft; a dulcimer with the undercut fingerboard that Homer made for his wife, Colista, about 1960 still hangs on the wall of Homer's den and is No. 739 of his 4,792 dulcimers. So it is obvious that the undercut fingerboard is one of his earlier innovations, not the creation of a foreign company that only in recent years has begun to capitalize on the traditional Appalachian dulcimer's growing popularity.

Such copying of Homer's design is sheer industrial intrigue and commercial infringement. When individual craftsmen copy Homer's work, on the other hand, the process may be seen as one of folkloric imitation, perhaps a modern counterpart of the older systems of familial or apprentice inheritance of traditional patterns. Unfortunately, however, the purely commercial interests often reflect little, if any, knowledge about the true traditionality of folkloric items, a fact glaringly revealed in their pseudo-instruments. For example, Homer bought and examined dulcimer imitations mass-produced by both South Korean and Czechoslovakian companies and, to his dismay, discovered them incapable of producing even an approximation of the sweet music characteristic of the traditional dulcimer; the sounds they did produce could only be called cacophonous. These dulcimers were fretted incorrectly—not one fret was in the proper position—and consequently could not be tuned, no matter where the bridge was moved; intonation, understandably, was terrible. In addition, the instruments were constructed almost totally of plywood. The Czechoslovakian dulcimer was advertised as rosewood, but Homer discovered that only the top layer was rosewood. The instrument also had metal gears like those on a guitar or banjo, a feature Homer considers not traditional.

Although Homer generally considers copying a compliment to his craftsmanship, he has taken legal steps to preclude copying of his dulcitar, a unique instrument developed entirely out of his own ingenuity and creative talents (fig. 8). Homer completed the construction of his first dulcitar early in 1971, just in time to exhibit it at the Berea arts and crafts fair (sponsored by the Kentucky Guild of Artists and Craftsmen) in May of that year. At the fair, a stranger became unusually interested in the new instrument and asked both Homer and Colista numerous questions about it. A few months later someone showed Homer an advertisement for a similar instrument, also called a dulcitar; upon investigation Homer discovered that the advertisement had been placed by the same individual who had so closely questioned him about his invention at the Berea fair.

Homer promptly secured the services of a patent attorney. Proof that the dulcitar was indeed Homer's creation finally came from the Smithsonian Institution and, indirectly, from my fieldwork. During the summer of 1971—soon after he had built the dulcitar—I visited Homer, and we discussed various aspects of his life and craft. These conversations were taped, and one of them dealt with the invention and characteristics of the dulcitar; also recorded on tape was Homer's discovery that the new instrument could be played to sound like the banjo. Subsequent to this fieldwork, in the late summer, I took one of Homer's dulcimers to the musical instruments division of the Smithsonian Institution and introduced Scott Odell, restoration specialist, and Cynthia Hoover, associate curator, to Homer's work. During our conversations I told them about the dulcitar, after which they contacted Homer and acquired some of his instruments for the Smithsonian's permanent and traveling collections, including a dulcitar; this early correspondence between the Smithsonian and Homer finally helped to prove that the dulcitar was indeed Homer's creation.

Homer is both humble and proud that the Smithsonian thought so highly of his work. His dulcitar and dulcimer are now represented in the Smithsonian's permanent collection, and his dulcitar was also placed in a traveling exhibit to illustrate innovation within traditional American folk craftsmanship. Homer has subsequently redesigned his brochure to include a short statement indicating the Smithsonian's recognition of his craft. Homer has every right to feel proud, for I know of no one for whom I have more respect in the field of musical instrument curatorship than Scott Odell, and I well remember Odell's first words when I showed him one of Homer's dulcimers; he said, "It's the finest, lightest dulcimer I've ever seen."

Much of our discussion concerned the fact that Homer's dulcimers are so finely finished that they exhibit what could nearly be called artwork rather then craftwork. Responding to questions concerning the distinction between "art" and "craft" in the making of his instruments, Homer's own comments, as usual, are trenchant:

The art comes in I suppose when you are designing, and using the pocketknife and actually carving to the finished line;
also, the tuning of the instrument I guess you would call an
art. Now my dulcimer is considered a craft, but my guitar
isn't, and yet the only difference is that the guitar has more
coats of finish and is rubbed out to a higher degree of fin-
ishing. . . . a dulcimer has never been made in a factory, but
the guitar certainly for many years has been a factory instrument, although there are people making them by hand and
have been ever since there was a guitar. But we think of a
guitar as a factory-made instrument. . . . Now custom work
itself borders on being art, and you can do the same kind of
custom work, say, for both a dulcimer and a guitar, but the
dulcimer itself is a craft while the guitar is not . . . I don't
think I could have joined the [Kentucky Artists and Craftsmen's Guild] as a guitar maker.

Homer feels that the traditional aspects of his dulcimer are still
maintained even when custom work is added. He says that custom
work of all kinds

actually was done by mountain craftsmen of former days. . . . I
believe it was Thomas who made about 1,500 instruments
in his lifetime, and he made every kind, fancy ones too; one
was sent to the Queen of England. (Whether that's true or not
I don't know; it is a story that has been around, but I've never
seen it written down.) Anyway, it was a common thing that
if you made anything for someone else, you might have done
a little bit extra for the particular individual; for example,
someone may have been religious and wanted a sound hole
shaped like a cross—what makes me say that is that I just
got an order for one like that. This custom thing is just as
traditional as anything else, I think.[42]

Homer is particularly conscious of the obligation to his craft to
remain a one-man operation. He emphatically states, "I have always
insisted that each and every dulcimer has only my personal attention, and I intend always to remain a one-man shop." He cites with
disdain an instance of a government-sponsored enterprise that set up
an assembly line production of "dulcimers" made of plywood, which
were sold as "mountain souvenirs;" this small factory turned out the
imitations at the rate of twenty to twenty-five per day, but even at

that rate of production, it eventually failed. Homer believes that people cannot be fooled with such products.

In contrast to such an assembly-line operation, Homer's *maximum* output is only one dulcimer per day—and that is assuming that all materials and tools are already available and that he works without interruption at top efficiency during all the daylight hours. He is quick to point out, too, that he could not at all maintain such a pace; his health, and eventually the quality of his work, would suffer. Although he is highly efficient, Homer says he is not a machine. He is fond of joking in pseudobraggadocio fashion about one of the "secrets" of his craftsmanship: at the first rough cutting, he says, he gets every piece of every instrument so close to the final measurement that he doesn't "throw anything away but the sawdust." Still, he is serious in maintaining that most top traditional Appalachian craftsmen of the past also strove to be efficient and economical; Homer considers this one mark of a fine traditional craftsman.

One technique that Homer has developed to improve the efficiency of his craft is to standardize as many dulcimer parts as possible. Doing so has not encroached upon the handcrafted quality of his instrument, however; rather, his standardization procedures and controls converge with his freehand work so effectively that truly remarkable overall uniformity in his handmade instruments is achieved; this is, to my mind, another mark of a fine craftsman. Certainly, older dulcimer makers like Thomas also adopted standardization procedures.

Perhaps the best example of the blending of Homer's standardization and his freehand craftsmanship can be seen in his dulcimer's fine rosewood pegs. One end of each peg is shaped by a tool of his own invention; the other is hand-carved, but each peg is still standardized. Homer says:

> The fingerboard . . . the top, and the back are fairly standardized—all have specific set measurements—so they all have to fit, but fitting the sides in is another question. . . . it is probably one of the hardest tasks of assembly. . . . I use patterns for each part, each time, for the top and back but not for the sides. . . . The pegbox and pegs are also somewhat standardized but require more hand carving than other parts. There is nothing mechanical about it, it's just that I happen to have worked out a system that will work well and save me time. . . . any peg I make will fit any of my dulcimers. It was really accidental; I didn't plan to do it but simply discovered

that it was so, then perfected it so that it would work as a standardized method.

In the pegs themselves and in Homer's method of crafting them can be seen the manner in which tradition, innovation, and society's modern tools have their respective but overlapping places within the revitalized but still traditional craft of dulcimer making. Once or twice someone has told Homer that the use of his peg former is not traditional, but Homer does not agree. Though it is true that such a device, being Homer's own invention, has no traditional heritage, it should be seen as having been developed within the traditional craft of dulcimer making; as scholar D.K. Wilgus asserts, "Despite all disclaimers, the folklorist is concerned with that which continues but changes."[43]

Another ingenious modification of his craft involves the homemade dulcimer clamps (they are, he claims, "the only kind that will do the job successfully") that Homer uses to hold the dulcimer all the way around its periphery when the sides are fitted in and glued—which, as mentioned earlier, Homer considers one of the most difficult steps in the final assembly process. The sides of Homer's dulcimers are set in; that is, the top and back of the dulcimer overhang the sides, as on a fiddle. Some craftsmen produce dulcimers with smooth sides and no overhanging back or top; that procedure requires less time and skill, as the side can be quickly glued to the top and back and the joints sanded smooth on a drum sander. Construction problems with the traditional inset sides have perennially plagued many dulcimer craftsmen, and repairs often involve the sides; however, Homer's ingenuity and expert craftsmanship have combined to perfect not only the mechanics of the dulcimer craft but also the dulcimer itself: in addition to making it a more durable instrument, his side assembly and construction methods (described in Part II) serve to enhance both the dulcimer's appearance and its musical quality.

Homer insists that preparing the parts of a dulcimer up to the point of final assembly is the most difficult and demanding part of his craft, both in time and knowledge. He says: "It is very time consuming to choose proper woods and to blend or match them, to shape them, sand them, and see to it that they will fit together well and make fine music." Homer's favorite wood for the sides and back of a dulcimer is black walnut, and often he is fortunate enough to find curly (or what he calls "feather-crotch") walnut, which does indeed produce an exquisite body. Homer is especially pleased when he succeeds in locating special or antique woods; he declares that it is extremely gratifying to a craftsman to be able to fabricate a fine instrument from such beautiful materials. Homer constantly scouts for such woods; for example, he obtained several yellow poplar beams from which he made dulcimer tops, from Berea College's Howard Hall when it was torn down during a reconstruction project; as Howard Hall was built in 1862, the beams were finely aged and largely without nail holes. He also acquired some yellow poplar from the pews of a country church that was razed, wood that was more than 150 years old. Often he has to bargain for choice materials. For example, the Howard Hall beams were nearly sold to someone who wanted to make fireplace mantels of them, but when Homer explained his intended use of the beams, everyone quickly agreed that to put this beautiful wood in Homer's instruments so that a great number of people could enjoy it—and in such a lovely way: by producing music—was far better than to use them for mantels in one person's home.

After obtaining the desired assortment, Homer then selects the right combination of different woods and plans how best to blend them together to make an instrument. His step-by-step construction procedure is detailed in Part II.

Homer quite obviously has very little time for handicrafts other than his dulcimer making. He does do some repair work, first for his own dulcimers (usually those that have been damaged by ill treatment) and then for nearly any sort of stringed instrument. People trust him with the most expensive of guitars, fiddles, and mandolins; indeed, the C.F. Martin Guitar Company asked him to become a Martin factory representative for repair of its instruments, but he declined; he does, however, represent Martin for sales in his area. When Homer does repair a Martin Instrument (even though not in an official capacity) the company still maintains the instrument's warranty, a confidence they do not extend indiscriminately to just any craftsman. His reputation has become so widespread that Homer has corresponded with, visited, or in some way dealt with many major manufacturers of stringed instruments, including Gibson. Also, because he is a truly creative craftsman, Homer often works intermittently on at least one other special instrument; for example, he recently completed, after nearly three years of painstaking effort, what may well prove to be his most finely wrought instrument, a mandolin (fig. 4). Considering the time, materials, and meticulous detail required in constructing this mandolin, Homer jokes that if he were to sell it (this instrument will not be sold; it is his personally), he might have to charge as much as $2,500 for it. The intricate custom inlay work on the instrument perhaps represents Homer's most elaborate artistry (see fig. 49, page 100); the actual cost of materials for the inlay alone approximated $1,200.

However, without question Homer's most innovative creations are the dulcitar—discussed earlier—and his newest experiment the dulcibro; to be sure, both are unique (figs. 8 and 9). Homer commented on the first dulcitar he completed:

> This is strictly an experimental instrument. . . . the only one in existence. It is a heart-shaped instrument with six strings, so you can play it like a guitar and a dulcimer both. . . . I didn't even know what I was making until my wife asked me one day when she saw me working on this thing—then I just said it was a 'dulcitar'. . . . It has a partial guitar neck but also combines a dulcimer scale. . . . The wood in the neck is over 150 years old. . . . Inside, it has a classic guitar structure, so I play it better as a guitar. The fingerboard is like a classic guitar up to the first five frets—chromatic—so that any key can be played. . . . I had to design it as I made it. It is patterned in part after a dulcimer that had a similar shape but not the heart shape in back. The construction is similar to a dulcimer except for the bracing inside, which is similar to classic guitar bracing so that the guitar sound can be achieved; of course the dulcimer didn't have the neck with five frets. The top is spruce, and is built in like the dulcimer.

Like his dulcitar, Homer's dulcibro is essentially a hybrid instrument, utilizing a basic dulcimer body in conjunction with the resonator cone characteristic of a dobro, hence the name. The dobro—probably not as familiar to the general public as the fiddle or the banjo or even the dulcimer—is an exotic version of the guitar, featuring a 12-inch-diameter concave resonator cone in combination with a raised string arrangement (four, six, or eight strings) to produce a sustained, ringing tonal quality reminiscent of the Hawaiian guitar. Originally devised by the Dopyeras brothers of California in the mid-twenties, the dobro was quite popular in the thirties, temporarily neglected in the late forties and early fifties, and then revived as a favorite instrument among old-time and bluegrass performers.[44] Homer, of course, was familiar with the instrument, liked its sound, and indeed owned one; consequently, in 1977 he began forming an idea of a new instrument that would combine some characteristics of the dobro with those of his own handcrafted dulcimer. Homer sketched a few of his ideas, but it was not until May of 1979 that he actually constructed

8. Homer's dulcitar

9. Homer's dulcibro

his first dulcibro. Built of rosewood, with a spruce top, Homer's dulcibro features a handmade aluminum cone—Homer could not buy the size of cone appropriate for a dulcimer so he made his own from printing press plates—and five strings, although he plans eventually to put on six. The strings make contact with the cone by means of a center screw in the dulcimer bridge. The result is an instrument that is played like a dulcimer but has both a dulcimer and a dobro tone.

If Homer's dulcitar and dulcibro represent his most innovative work, it is surely his dulcimer that best represents Homer's expertise with traditional crafts. As Homer himself has said, it required many years of experience to realize the high degree of excellence manifest in his dulcimer. Those years of experience provided Homer the opportunity to experiment with and time to perfect the innumerable processes involved in each step of the construction. Perhaps the following section, describing in step-by-step detail the intricacies of Homer's craft, will help to demonstrate just how meticulous and painstaking Homer must be in crafting and constructing his dulcimer. Also included are a detailed discussion of Homer's custom work (such as mother-of-pearl inlay), his advice on the care and repair of dulcimers, his tuning system, and other information that Homer has accumulated over the years that should benefit any dulcimer owner.

II
THE ANATOMY
OF THE LEDFORD
DULCIMER

To create a visually aesthetic instrument, dulcimer woods can be variously combined. For example, a dark green top of yellow poplar handsomely complements a balck walnut body; a cherry body is attractive with a spruce or white pine top (yellow poplar, however, does not complement cherry); likewise, a mahogany body blends well with a top of spruce or white pine, or indeed any member of the pine family; and a redwood top goes well with a black walnut body, whereas it will clash with cherry. Homer believes that it is preferable not to stain the woods, but rather to retain their natural coloring. Homer also warns that dulcimers should not be constructed of only one type of wood: if one of the relatively soft woods is used throughout the instrument, the back and sides will be fragile and vulnerable to bruises, scratches, and nicks; if a hard wood is used throughout, the sound of the instrument will be adversely affected.

Whichever woods are chosen, all should be thoroughly dried, preferably kiln-dried, stock. These woods may be purchased—in a rough state, of course—at a local lumberyard; they may vary in length from 30 inches to 10 or 12 feet ("shorts"—boards no longer than seven feet—are preferable) and should be one to two inches thick and about eight inches wide, although wider stock can be cut down to proper size. Wood should be selected, first of all, for tone. If a board of, say, black walnut is especially heavy, the wood is too hard for dulcimer construction—it will not vibrate freely. Homer advises that after some experience, the craftsman will be able to determine the desired weight of a board by merely lifting it.

If possible, selected woods should exhibit attractive grains or figures, a characteristic that is rather difficult to obtain in black walnut; however, if such a piece of black walnut is located, but is a bit too hard, it can still be used by compensating for sound with the use of softer woods in the top and sides. A small knot in the wood will not preclude its use in the dulcimer back or sides as long as it will still bend; however, highly figured woods, such as curly maple or walnut, must be specially treated (as described in the assembly section) before they can be used in dulcimer sides.

Wood for the dulcimer top or soundboard is chosen primarily for purity of line—the way the grain runs; Homer says that quarter-sawed spruce, which can be purchased from a musical instrument supply house, is particularly beautiful for the soundboard. This wood has been cut in such a way that the annual rings, when viewed from the end of the board, appear to stand vertically. Because quarter-sawed boards are stronger and less likely to warp than slab-cut lumber—where the rings appear almost parallel with the surface of the board—

SELECTING THE WOOD

Homer states that in the construction of a traditio
dulcimer, the selection of the proper woods is the
uisite for building a superior instrument. For the
Homer recommends the harder woods, such as blac
and mahogany. Black walnut is particularly suita
bodies because it glues well, it is attractive and prov
and dulcimer owners apparently often prefer it. Bot
the end block should be constructed of the same ma
of the instrument—not only so that the coloring of
be pleasing to the eye, but also because harder wo
to the proper functioning of these two components.
soft wood, such as poplar or pine, is used for the
will wear away the wood, causing both the pegs a
tached to them to slip continually; in the end block,
bury themselves in soft wood, thereby quickly lc

For the dulcimer top, or soundboard, softer ai
resonant woods—such as yellow poplar, butternu
pine, and spruce—are recommended; these woods
the sound frequencies of the plucked strings and
dulcimer its characteristic soft, sweet sound.

The fingerboard of the dulcimer presents a s
it must be constructed of material which is both ri
the string is pushed down onto the fingerboard, t
vibrate—and at the same time able to transmit th
string to the tone chamber, allowing the string t
meet these requirements, a soft wood can be use
tion of the fingerboard can be laminated to create
preferably, the fingerboard can be constructed of
as black walnut, and its underside hollowed out
of it touch the dulcimer body. This hollowing o
also helps prevent the fingerboard from warping,
the instrument's musical quality.

For the dulcimer pegs and bridge, Homer rec
rosewood, if available. Although less expensive th
of wood—such as ebony—rosewood produces a pe
for the dulcimer; and the wood has a natural oil
peg, preventing it from popping and squeaking wl
ing it to turn smoothly and tune more accurate
wood cannot be secured, however, Indian ro
although the latter is prone to cracking—can b
wood or ebony can also be used for the dulcime

they are preferable for musical instruments. However, if poplar or pine is used for the soundboard, it does not necessarily have to be quarter-sawed.

Because of the sweet, mellow sound they produce, antique woods—one hundred years old or more—are particularly excellent construction materials for dulcimers.

CUTTING AND SHAPING THE COMPONENTS

Tops and Backs. Each board must be individually smoothed down and resawed before construction can begin. Homer first runs both sides of the board across a jointer. Next, he uses a table saw with a hollow-ground or planer blade—which will cut smoothly to nearly exact thickness—to saw the board to the proper thickness for a dulcimer top or back. If the wood is cut too thin, it will be so structurally weak that a thumb can be pushed through it; if too thick, it will not vibrate freely but produce a shrill rather than a sweet sound.

The fence of the table saw is pulled to within 1/8 inch of the blade (or, with some softer woods, 3/32 inch but never more), the approximate thickness of a guitar top. Then the board is set on its edge, run through the saw, turned over and set on its opposite edge, and run through the machine a second time. As the board used for dulcimer tops and backs must be approximately 7 inches wide at this state, two passes of the 10-inch blade of the table saw, which cuts to a depth of about three inches, will not slice quite all the way through the wood; consequently, the piece in the center must be freed with either a band saw or a handsaw. This completes what is called the slabbing or sawing-off process; if well done, it will produce a relatively smooth board and minimize the need for sanding.

If more than one dulcimer is to be constructed, several pieces for tops and backs may be prepared at one time. In that case, it is best to match each top with a back, and identify each pair; for example, the insides of two boards—the sides that will be the interior of the instrument—can be marked with a pencil, say with an "A" on a top and an "A" on a back. Then, with insides facing, the pairs are fastened together at each end with either glue or staples (this area is later cut off); in this way, the top and back of a dulcimer can later be cut to identical shape and size. Finally, the paired tops and backs should be neatly stacked until there are enough to make several dulcimers. Homer often prepares seven pairs of boards at one time—enough for one to two weeks' work.

To shape the pair of boards, a plywood pattern is placed on top and Homer traces around it (fig. 10) with a pencil or ball-point pen (the latter's marking is easier to see). The paired top and back are then cut *at one time* with the board bearing the outline lying uppermost, of course, so the pattern can be followed. First, the boards are roughly cut to pattern with a band saw; then they are further shaped down, by hand, with a felt block wrapped in 150-grade sandpaper. The felt block is approximately 2 1/2 inches thick and 4 inches long and has a rounded top surface; when this block is pressed down against the wood and rubbed back and forth in a sanding motion, total contact between the two is achieved. When the edges of the boards have been sanded smooth and even, only then can the boards be taken apart. If the shaping process is not completed in this fashion—that is, treating the boards as a pair—it is possible that the dulcimer top and back may not match.

After the pieces have been separated, the back is ready for more sanding. Because the interior surfaces of the dulcimer will not be visible when the instrument is completed, they need only be smooth, not finely finished; therefore, Homer sands them just once, with 100-grade sandpaper. The outside surfaces, however, are sanded twice: at this stage with 150-grade, and then—after assembly—with 220-grade sandpaper. When the back has had its first sanding inside and out, and its edges have been gently rounded, it is ready for assembly; the top must first have sound holes cut into it.

Homer uses a router to cut the sound holes and prefers to do so before sanding, as the grit that becomes embedded in sanded wood could dull the router blade. (The same precaution applies to using the jointer; that is, it is preferable not to run a sanded board over the jointer—the effect is similar to that of cutting through sandpaper. Cutting a sanded board does less damage to the table saw, which has sharp teeth instead of one blade: the teeth of the table saw can be filed, but the blades of the jointer and router must be ground. In recent years, however, as new and tougher materials have been used for machine blades—there are carbide-tipped router blades, for example—this prohibition is not as imperative as it once was, and Homer now sometimes sands before using power tools.) An aluminum template, into which the desired shape of the sound hole has been cut, is positioned over the outside of the top, and Homer traces the hole's outline on the wood (fig. 11).

Sound holes must be placed in the center of the bend in both the lower and upper bouts (the *bouts* of a dulcimer are the bulges at either end of the instrument; the narrower area between the bouts is called the *waist*). As collars or guides are common accessories to the router, a guide can be used with the tool to form each hole perfectly. If more than one shape of sound hole is wanted, additional patterns must be designed.

After all the holes are cut, the inside and outside of the top are sanded as was done with the back, and the top is also ready for assembly.

10. Tracing pattern of dulcimer top

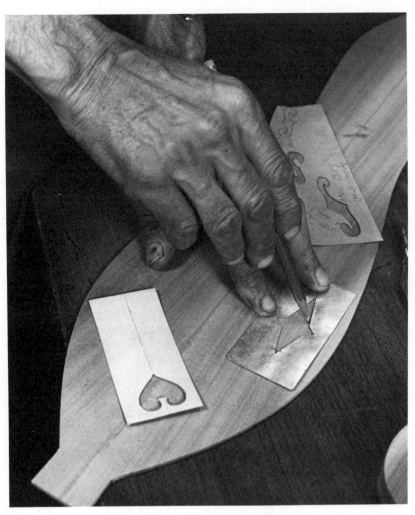

11. Tracing pattern of sound hole

Sides. After running both surfaces of a rough board across a jointer, Homer cuts the sides of the dulcimer on a table saw so that each one measures 1/8 inch thick, approximately 1 1/2 inches wide (this dimension—the depth of the instrument—varies with different woods and different dulcimer styles), and about 29 inches long; the side can be shortened at a later stage in the construction if need be. Like the top and back, the sides are sanded with 100-grade sandpaper on the inside and 150-grade on the outside; these outer surfaces, too, will be sanded later with 220-grade sandpaper to achieve the smoothest possible finish.

Pegboxes. Again using a jointer, Homer smooths down both sides of a board until it is 1 3/8 inches thick. A plywood pattern of the pegbox is placed on the board and traced, and the shape is cut out with a band saw. Using a 5/16-inch bit, the holes for the pegs are drilled as indicated by the pattern—three holes for a three-string dulcimer, and four for a four-string (fig. 12). Then, after the initial drilling, a violin type of reamer is inserted into the drill press to ream the peg holes so that they will perfectly fit the tapered pegs.

Next, the area in which the strings are to be wound within the pegbox must be hollowed out, first with a Forsner bit and drill press, and then more carefully with Homer's specially made chisel or a pocketknife. The size of this hollow in the pegbox varies according to the style of the instrument, the number of pegs, how the peghead is carved, and other considerations; the pegs must be far enough apart to allow room for the fingers to turn them. The Forsner bit has a very small center tip, and because of the stabilizing effect of the bottom knife edge—which goes almost all the way around the bit and cuts ahead of the main chipper cutter—the bit can make a fairly smooth-bottomed hole. Homer then uses his pocketknife, or his homemade chisel—made from a half-round gouge-type metal file—to complete the scooping-out process. When the hole is about 1 1/4 inches deep, 3 3/8 inches long, and 5/8 inch wide, its sides and particularly its bottom must be smoothed with either a file or a half-round wood rasp.

Three cuts are then made in the pegbox: a notch for the fingerboard and two slots for the sides. The notch that will receive the end of the fingerboard is cut with a band saw and is about 1 3/8 inches wide (the width of the end of the pegbox), 3/4 inch high (or the height of the fingerboard plus the top), and 1/4 inch deep. The slots into which the sides will fit are cut on either side of the pegbox below the recess for the fingerboard, in the end portion of the pegbox which has not been cut away; the slots are approximately 1/4 inch from the recess so that the fingerboard, when it is positioned in the recess, overhangs the slots by about 1/4 inch (fig. 13). These two slots must be cut at a 30° angle and approximately 1/8 inch wide, 1/4 inch deep, and 1 1/2 inches long. They can be cut slightly deeper—as are the slots in the end block—as long as they are not visible from the top of the pegbox where the fingerboard fits.

Because the sides of the dulcimer are put into place last, it is extremely important to cut these slots that receive the sides as accurately as possible or the dulcimer will not fit together properly. For this reason Homer uses a table saw, as this machine enables him to cut the angle of the slots precisely; also, he can utilize the fence on the table saw so that the blade will not wander. The pegbox block is set on end, backed up with a block to prevent it from splintering, and run through the table saw, which is tilted at a 30 ° angle; this is done on each side. Finally, the pegbox is sanded, first with 150-grade and then with 220-grade sandpaper, and then put aside until assembly. If desired, several pegboxes may be constructed at one time and stored.

12. Drilling peg holes in pegbox

13. Pegbox slots to
   receive sides

End Blocks. The end block, a rectangular block at the end of the dulcimer opposite the pegbox, is cut on the table saw according to a plywood pattern (fig. 14) and is approximately three inches high, 1 3/8 inches wide (the same width as the pegbox), and 1 1/2 inches long. Like the pegbox, the end block contains two slots into which the ends of the dulcimer sides will fit. These slots, too, are cut at a 30° angle 1/4 inch from the recess for the fingerboard, so that the fingerboard, when it is positioned in the recess, overlaps the slots by about 1/4 inch. Much as were the slots for the pegbox, the slots in the end block are cut on the table saw with a 1/8 inch-wide blade, making the slot slightly larger than 1/8 inch wide, 1 1/2 inches long, and 1/4 inch deep (fig. 15); the end block's slots are made slightly over-sized so that the dulcimer sides will fit into them somewhat loosely, and then, should the sides swell in humid weather, they will have room to expand without cracking either themselves or the end block, or kicking loose various joints in the dulcimer.

The end block must also have a section cut away, to receive the fingerboard and top; the procedure is identical to that used for the pegbox. Moreover, the end block must be notched to hold the ball end of the strings. This notch is cut in the back end of the end block, about 1/2 inch down from the top; then three or four holes—depending on the number of strings—are drilled through the notch (fig. 16).

Not only does this notch partially hide the ball ends of the strings, it also holds the strings solidly so that they will more readily remain in tune and it allows the use of an adjustable bridge under the strings. On some other makers' dulcimers (and Homer's earliest ones), pegs—around which the string's ends are looped—are used in place of the notch (fig. 17). However, both pegs and loops tend to give or loosen, thus allowing the strings to slacken; consequently, Homer prefers the notch. After the notches and slots are cut and the holes drilled, the end block can be sanded and put aside until assembly. Again, several end blocks may be made at one time.

14. Tracing pattern of end block

15 (*above*). End-block slots to receive sides

16 (*right*). Notch in end block for balled end of strings

17. Old-style end-block assembly with stationary bridge

Fingerboards. To prevent warping, the dulcimer fingerboard must be ripped out of the straightest possible stock, and it must be ripped down—that is, sawed parallel to the grain—two times. First, using the table saw and a hollow-ground blade that cuts to a smooth finish, Homer rips the board fairly close to its final dimensions—1 3/8 inches wide, 27 1/2 inches long, and 3/4 inch deep (this will vary somewhat); then he runs it across the jointer to make it straight, smooth, and even. Next, the fingerboard is again run through the table saw and cut even closer to dimension. Finally, the jointer is used a second time to remove just enough from all surfaces to bring the fingerboard to exact specification.

After this procedure, the fingerboard will usually remain straight; that it does not warp is extremely important, because if the fingerboard becomes crooked, the dulcimer cannot be played. Unfortunately, it is impossible to control warping absolutely, and a fingerboard can warp even after being put on a dulcimer. Usually, the harder the wood, the more likely it is to warp; for example, walnut is a relatively hard wood and therefore more likely to warp than butternut, a relatively soft wood. An exception to this generalization is mahogany which, though a hard wood, will scarcely warp at all because it comes from such large trees. Thanks to the particular care he takes in wood selection and construction, Homer's fingerboards rarely present any problems.

After the fingerboard has been ripped out perfectly straight, a portion of it near the end block—approximately six inches long, 3/8 inch deep, and across the entire 1 3/8 inch width—must be cut out with a band saw so that when the instrument is strummed, the player's pick or fingers will clear the fingerboard (see the sketch on page 24); otherwise, the player would be strumming the fingerboard as well as the strings.

Next, a slot is cut—preferably with a dado head, but a table saw blade can be used—into the underside of the fingerboard (fig. 18). Its size increases in proportion to the hardness of the wood; that is, if the fingerboard is walnut, the slot is made 12 to 18 inches long, 1/2 inch wide, and 3/8 inch deep; if butternut, a slightly shallower slot is needed. When the fingerboard is placed on the top of the dulcimer, the slot provides a dead air space between the dulcimer top and the fingerboard; it therefore acts as an insulator and also helps prevent the fingerboard from warping.

Homer states that, contrary to some opinions, such a hollow is not part of the dulcimer tone chamber, nor does it affect the sound to any great extent; in the anatomy of Homer's dulcimer, the primary function of the hollow fingerboard is structural, not tonal.

Once the fingerboard has been shaped, the places where the nut, the bridge, and the frets will go must be marked on it. After several years of experimenting, Homer has standardized his dulcimer scale; as recently as 1977, he transferred this scale onto a piece of lucite cut to the exact length of the fingerboard and inserted brass brads through the lucite at the exact positions of the nut, the bridge, and each fret. Consequently, all Homer now has to do is to lay the lucite scale on top of the fingerboard and tap it with a light hammer so that the brads will make small indentations in the fingerboard, marking the positions of the bridge, the nut, and the holes for each of the staple-type frets (fig. 19).

A standard scale can be worked out on a mathematical formula called the 18 formula; the length of the scale—that is the distance from the bridge to the nut—is divided by 18, determining the position of the first fret; then the distance from the first fret to the bridge is measured and divided by 18 again, determining the position of the second fret; this process is continued until all 14 frets are positioned.

Although the 18 formula scale is utilized by many reputable dulcimer craftsmen, Homer feels that his standardized scale—which he set up by ear—is more accurate than the 18 formula scale and assures that all notes on his dulcimer will harmonize reasonably well with notes on other instruments. Dulcimer craftsmen of long ago also set up scales by ear, but they were often inaccurate; indeed, the frets on very old dulcimers usually have been moved one or more times in an endeavor to correct the scale. As Homer says, "Their scales were evidently only as good as their ears, and you know when it comes to music, some people's ears just aren't too good." (Also no doubt partly because of the difficulty they experienced with the musical aspects of their craft, many old-time dulcimer makers used frets under only *one* string; that is, a player could note only one string. Of course, such dulcimers were quite easy to play, no doubt another reason for the one fretted string.) Proper apportionment of scale seemingly was an elusive goal for most early craftsmen and is also a subject of some disagreement among modern dulcimer makers. It is agreed that the scale is diatonic—there are no sharps or flats—but craftsmen differ in their opinions concerning the placement of the first fret; some believe that the distance between the first fret and the nut should be greater than the distance between the second fret and the third fret, and if the dulcimer scale is computed mathematically rather than by ear, such an apportionment of the scale, in Homer's opinion, is preferable. It should be remembered, however, that there is no perfect scale.

Homer has standardized the dulcimer scale to his own satisfaction, however, so after marking the fingerboard, he uses a pocketknife or a triangular file to make a small slot crosswise in its pegbox end where the nut will later be inserted; it should be cut according to the size of the nut to be used (fig. 20). Next, Homer marks each fret position with a very fine line, using either a pocketknife or an awl called a scriber (the latter can be purchased or specially made by sharpening the point of a nail set—the punch used to countersink nails—to a scriber taper).

If traditional staple-type frets are to be used, Homer punches the holes for them in the fingerboard at this time, using a nail punch or an awl that he has, again, adapted from a nail set (fig. 21); the staple frets themselves are not put into the fingerboard until the dulcimer is completely assembled. For mandolin- or guitar-type frets, however (which some customers insist on), small slots—roughly 1/16 inch deep—are cut all the way across the fingerboard with a fretsaw (fig. 22). The mandolin frets are cut with plier snippers from German or nickel silver (an alloy formulated specifically for the purpose) to the precise length—1 3/8 inches—of the slot (the width of the fingerboard) and driven into the slots with a soft brass- or plastic-headed hammer; they should be driven all the way down so that just their tops protrude above the fingerboard. Care should be taken that the frets enter the wood vertically; to facilitate this, the fingerboard should be placed on a level metal surface, such as the machine surface of the table saw, while the frets are inserted. Then the fingerboard may be sanded and put aside, ready for assembly. Like other parts of the dulcimer, several fingerboards may be prepared at one time.

18. Under side of hollowed-out fingerboard

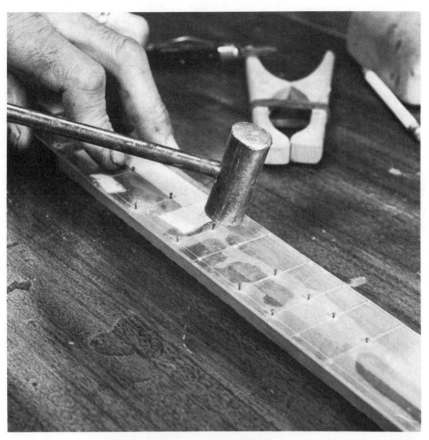

19 (above). Using lucite scale to mark fret, nut, and bridge positions

20 (below). Slot in fingerboard for nut

21 (above). Punching holes for staple-type frets
22 (below). Using fretsaw to make grooves for guitar-type frets

Pegs. Brazilian rosewood, if available, is the preferred wood for pegs, although ebony or Indian rosewood will serve. Using a plywood pattern and a pencil, Homer traces the shape of a peg on a piece of wood preferably 6 but at least 4 inches thick so that he can make a number of pegs at one time. Homer saws around the outline of the pattern with a band saw, then lays the peg shaped piece flat down on the band saw and rips off as many pegs as possible, allowing a 3/8-inch thickness for each peg. Each piece should be cut as closely to the finished size as possible to prevent wasting both wood and time.

After the pegs have been band-sawed, Homer uses a pocketknife and a sanding disk to round off each peg stem. The head of each peg must now be shaped so that it will have a little scalloped-out place to fit the fingers. This is done on a special sanding drum wrapped with two grades of sandpaper or beltings, one coarse (80D-grade) and the other fine (150-grade). The peg is laid on the drum, which scallops out both sides of the peg to approximately the desired depth (fig. 23). The peg is then sanded by hand and gently polished on fine sandpaper belting. The stems of the pegs are also further shaped in a specially designed trimmer that is Homer's own invention; also made of rosewood, it resembles a giant pencil sharpener. The peg is inserted into the trimmer and turned against an adjustable cutting blade until it is perfectly round and tapered to fit the holes previously reamed in the pegbox (fig. 24). To guarantee that the tapers of the pegs and holes will match, Homer made the hole in the trimmer with the same reamer that he uses for the holes in the pegbox. After the stem of

23. Shaping peg on sanding drum

each peg is trimmed, he whittles around the edge of the head with his pocketknife, leaving it rounded and with a chipped effect (fig. 25).

The peg is then completed except for buffing the head or spraying it with a flat lacquer. If lacquer is accidentally sprayed onto the stem, however, the peg must be replaced in the trimmer and turned one time to skim off the lacquer, since a slick or polished stem will slip in the pegbox hole. Homer recently devised a way to avoid this problem; he has reamed pegholes into a long board, deep enough so that when pegs are placed in the holes, only their tops protrude. Using this board, Homer is able to spray the heads of the pegs without getting lacquer on the stems (fig. 26)—a far more efficient and less time-consuming method than wrapping protective tape around each stem, as he used to do.

Finally, Homer inspects the pegs one by one and, while doing so, turns the tapered end gently one time in a piece of sandpaper, thus providing it with a "grip" to assure that it will not slip when in its pegbox hole. (If the dulcimer is given any care at all, a peg constructed in this manner should hold the string securely for four or five years without being resanded.) The pegs are then put aside to await final assembly of the dulcimer.

24. Using peg trimmer to shape peg stem

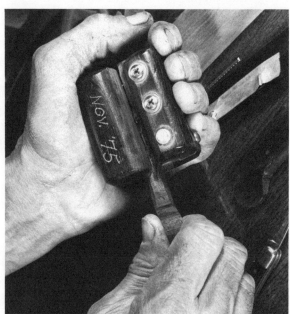

25 (*above*). Carving scalloped peg head

26 (*right*). Pegs positioned in board for lacquering

Bridge. The Ledford dulcimer's adjustable bridge is cut from rosewood or ebony; it measures 1/4 inch high, 1/4 inch thick, and approximately the length of the width of the fingerboard—about 1 3/8 inches—although it may be as much as 1/8 inch shorter. The bridge must be at least 1/4 inch high so that if the player wishes to play fast or lively tunes on the instrument, the strings will not "buzz" on the frets; if the bridge were lower and a player pressed down on, say, the third fret, the string might "buzz" on the fourth. Also, it is much easier to lower a high bridge—by deepening the notches for the strings—than to raise a low bridge.

Several bridges may be cut out at one time. First, a strip of rosewood or ebony is ripped out on the table saw, using a planer blade, and then cut lengthwise on the band saw. Notches for the strings are made with a pocketknife or file.

Nut. The dulcimer nut is constructed of rosewood, ebony, ivory, or some other fine material. The dimensions of the nut may vary somewhat, but in general it is 1/4 inch wide, 3/16 inch thick, and a little longer than the fingerboard is wide. Homer rips the nut from rosewood or ebony stock with the table saw; or, if he chooses ivory, he purchases it already cut, with a diamond saw, to the dimensions that he requires. A small slot for each string must be made in the nut with a triangular file or a pocketknife—deep enough so that the string will bury itself in the notch; that is, after the dulcimer is assembled, the craftsman should be able to lay a straight edge across the nut without touching the strings.

ASSEMBLY

First, Homer clamps a fingerboard to a dulcimer top; he then cuts the top off at both ends to make it exactly the length of the fingerboard (fig. 27). After ascertaining that top and fingerboard are perfectly aligned, he removes the clamps. Aliphatic glue (white polyvinyl glue was Homer's choice before the new aliphatic glue was developed) is used—as it is throughout the entire assembly, except for the sides—to secure one end of the top to an end block and the other to a pegbox. Next, glue is applied to the underside of the fingerboard, along the edges of its hollowed-out recess, and on both ends. The fingerboard is then positioned upon the top between the pegbox and the end block (fig. 28), and it should fit perfectly. After the end block, pegbox, and fingerboard have been glued to the dulcimer top, a wooden block is C-clamped at each end of the top; the block is approximately 1 3/8 inches long (the width of the tapered narrow end of the top), 1/2 inch thick, and at least as wide as the C-clamp, preferably wider. Then the glue is allowed to dry for at least thirty minutes; the pressure of the C-clamps and wooden blocks should assure a solid bond between the glued parts (fig. 29). If Homer desires to continue immediately with assembly, rather than waiting half an hour, he can tack 1/4-inch brads from the underside of the top into the fingerboard; these brads will not be visible on the finished instrument but will hold the fingerboard against the top and, in combination with the C-clamps, allow assembly to continue immediately. However, a better result is obtained if the glue is allowed to dry before continuing.

Next, glue is applied to the bottom surfaces of the pegbox and the end block; then the back of the dulcimer is glued to them and, at the same time, aligned with the top. To hold the back against the pegbox and end block while the glue is drying, Homer must use clamps (wire brads would be visible on the outside of the dulcimer) and set it aside for 30 minutes. The back will, at this point, be too long for the rest of the instrument (fig. 30); however, it need not be trimmed until the assembly is completed.

Once the glue is dry, a gummed identification label may be placed inside the dulcimer, secured to the back so that it is visible through one of the sound holes in the top; this label may display the name of the craftsman; the warranty and serial number; and, if antique woods are used, their age and source—plus any other information the individual craftsman may desire. Such a label is characteristic of the traditional Appalachian dulcimer. To identify his very first dulcimers, Homer merely signed his name with a pencil on the inside of the back. After he returned to Tennessee from the John C. Campbell Folk School, he whittled his own name stamp out of red cedar and dipped it in ink to make the impression on the inside of his dulcimers (Homer recalls in amusement that the first stamp he so painstakingly carved rendered his name backwards; hence he had to start over and make another). Later still, he wrote or typed his name and address on a piece of brown paper tape which he glued into his dulcimers, but since sometime in the early 1960s—he is unsure of the date—Homer has used a printed identification label (fig. 31). He has also been putting serial numbers on his label for several years; he has accurate records on nearly all of the dulcimers he has made, and has assigned numbers to them since about 1949, but he has entered the serial number on the identification label only in recent years. Some of his early dulcimers have been sent back to Homer with the request by the owner that he install an identification label; sometimes specific information—such as the kind of wood, date of construction, and serial number—is asked for, and Homer has always obliged when he could provide the facts.

At some point in the assembly process, usually before the sides are installed—so that he can maintain better control over the process—Homer scribes a fine line (somewhat similar to purfling on a violin) around the edges of the dulcimer top and back. For this procedure he uses his own invented tool, which is actually a nail bent into a U-shape at the pointed end. He merely holds the nail against the edge of the wood so that the bent tip scribes an even and continuous line, and runs it around the entire border of both top and back (fig. 32).

The next step is to attach the sides of the instrument to the top and back. Unlike numerous other dulcimer craftsmen, Homer does not usually steam or heat his dulcimer sides before inserting them. However, when using figured woods such as curly maple or walnut or cherry, in which the grain of the wood does not run straight and therefore makes the wood vulnerable to breakage, Homer does advocate heating or steaming the dulcimer side before bending it into place. Depending upon the grain of the wood, the angle of the bend, and the skill of the craftsman, the dulcimer side can be merely heated and then attached, or it can be soaked in water and then heated to make steam. If figured wood has to bend only slightly, it sometimes can be bent dry, but generally, at least heating is desirable. However, as indicated, the heating or steaming process is not necessary with other than figured wood.

Before attaching the dulcimer sides to the top and the back, Homer first verifies the correct length of each side via a "dry run." Beginning at the pegbox end—which has the sharper bend, or bout, and therefore demands more careful attention—Homer first inserts one end of a side into the 30° angle slot. Then the side is fitted between the top and the back in the following manner: the strip is bent slightly, secured with one of Homer's homemade violin-type clamps (see page 105), bent slightly again, clamped again, and so on (fig. 33); this is continued, with the clamps placed side by side, until the opposite end of the strip can be inserted into the receiving slot in the end block. Usually about 18 clamps will be needed to complete this process.

If during the dry run the side fits in all respects, it is removed; Weldwood glue is spread on both edges and ends; and the entire bending and clamping procedure is repeated (fig. 34). If the dry run reveals that the side is too long, it can be trimmed to the proper length. Actually, it is preferable for the side to be just a fraction too long and too wide so that its ends and sides can be sanded down very slightly for a good tight fit between the top and back and in the two end slots. Obviously, however, if the side is too short or too narrow, it must be replaced.

Because the top and back of Homer's dulcimer overhang the sides, the side strips are placed approximately 1/16 inch inside the edges of the top and back. This measurement does not need to be exact; indeed, it is not measured but only estimated. It does not matter if the side is indented a little less or a little more than 1/16 inch, or if the indentation is not perfectly even the entire length of the side, as long as the jointure is attractive to the eye. Actually, Homer says, perfection in this particular matter is not even desirable, as it would cause the dulcimer to appear machine made rather than handcrafted.

As indicated, Weldwood glue rather than aliphatic or white glue is used when fitting in the sides. A plastic resin glue in powder form, Weldwood need only be mixed with water; it is used for the sides because it dries more slowly than aliphatic or white glue and allows Homer ample time to insert the sides before it sets up. After the side has been fitted in and clamped, all excess glue must be removed while it is still wet; Homer uses a damp cloth and a round ebony stick, about the size of a No. 6 nail, with a sharp-pointed end. If the excess glue is allowed to dry on the dulcimer, it will set as hard as concrete and be exceedingly difficult to remove.

The second side is inserted between the top and back in the same manner as the first, including the dry run. A difficulty with the second side, which is not experienced with the first, occurs when it must finally be inserted into the end block slot. Because the first side is in place at this point, Homer cannot put his hand inside the dulcimer to guide the second side into the end block slot or to push the strip out should it slip in too far between the top and the back of the dulcimer; nor can he easily retrieve the side should it slip completely to the bottom of the slot. The 30° angle slot, as already stated, must be slightly larger than the end of the side which fits into it to allow for expansion of the wood under humid conditions; the side must not go all the way down in, for there must be just a little bit of space left to serve as an expansion joint. Therefore, some method must be devised to guide the end of the second side into the end block slot, yet prevent its slipping to the bottom.

Homer uses the following procedure: after the side has been clamped up to the last bend of the dulcimer—within six inches of the end—he inserts a pocketknife blade into the slot and sticks the knife into the wood until it will not slip (fig. 35); this will not mar the dulcimer—a little nick will merely be left in the bottom of the slot which, of course, is not visible. Homer then bends the side and puts the end of it against the blade of the pocketknife; in this position, the knife is pushing against the side so it cannot go into the slot until the knife blade is removed. With his left hand, Homer holds the outside of the dulcimer top and back firmly and fairly tightly, thus preventing the side from slipping when the knife blade is removed; he then slowly removes the blade, at the same time holding onto the side with a couple of fingers, until the end of the strip can be eased into the slot. When the side is almost—but not quite—in position, it is clamped at the very end, tightly enough to prevent it from slipping into the slot any farther, but loosely enough to permit it to be pushed. Then, carefully and gradually, Homer pushes the side down with his thumb until the top and back are overhanging approximately 1/16 inch.

Homer can then tighten the end clamp, put on three or four additional clamps, clean off the excess glue, and put the body aside for approximately four hours. (To speed up production, the dulcimer can be placed about two feet in front of a small—5,000-BTU—gas or electric heater, which will speed-dry the glue in about an hour. In the summer the same result can be achieved by placing the dulcimer in a large cardboard box and setting it in the sun; Homer often uses this "solar oven," which is his own idea.)

27. Cutting off ends of top even with fingerboard

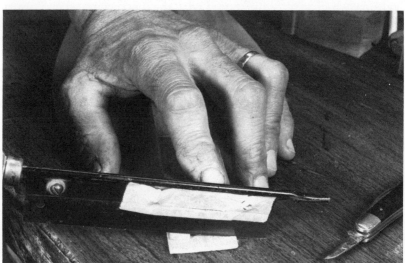

28 (*right*). Positioning fingerboard between pegbox and end block

29 (*below*). Clamp holding glued parts together

30 (*above*).
Positioning
back before
sawing flush

31 (*left*). Affixing
maker's card to
inside of back

32. Using bent nail to create purfling

33 *(right)*. Using homemade clamps to install sides

34 *(below)*. Homemade clamps holding sides until glue dries

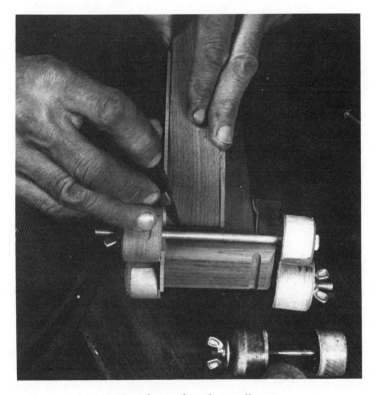

35. Completing the side installation

TRIMMING AND FINISHING

After the glue is dry, the clamps should be removed from the assembled instrument. As stated earlier, the dulcimer back is longer than the rest of the assembled instrument, so it must now be trimmed to the proper length; the extended ends are cut off with a coping saw so that the end block and pegbox ends are flush with the ends of the back (fig. 36). Then Homer uses his pocketknife to trim and gently round off all edges of the dulcimer that are designed to be flush (fig. 37); the top and back, it must be remembered, overhang the sides.

When all trimming is completed, any nicks or slight cracks in the wood—and there are usually a few—or gaps in the joints may be filled and smoothed over with wood putty, which must, of course, match the color of the wood so the repair will not be conspicuous. Homer makes his own matching putty by taking extremely fine sanding dust from the same material as that to be filled—for example, to repair a slight crack in black walnut, he uses black walnut sanding dust—and mixing it with a clear plastic household cement; the resultant putty will dry and be ready to sand within ten minutes.

Finally, Homer sands the entire dulcimer with 220-grade sandpaper; this fine-sanding makes the surface of the dulcimer relatively slick and provides an excellent base for the finish.

Various finishes may be used on a dulcimer—for example, boiled linseed oil, tung oil, or lacquer; the choice depends upon the preference of the individual craftsman. Homer is convinced that the best finish for the protection and tone of a dulcimer is a clear, flat spraying lacquer (which, he says, is superior to brushing lacquer); the spray dries quickly to a nonglossy finish, it is durable, and many good commercial brands are available. Homer uses Sherwin-Williams Sherwood Dull Lacquer; he believes that the substance added to make it dull does not settle in the container as quickly as it does in other brands, and therefore the lacquer does not need to be agitated continually.

Before the spraying is done, the top surface of the fingerboard, where a lacquer finish is not wanted, is covered with masking tape or boiled linseed oil. If mandolin- or guitar-type frets have already been installed on the fingerboard, masking tape is preferable; with traditional staple-type frets, which will *not* yet have been installed, either tape or linseed oil may be used on the still smooth and even surface. After the fingerboard is covered, Homer sprays the entire dulcimer with a coat of sanding sealer, a product which is recommended for use with the lacquer. The sealer is allowed to dry for approximately thirty minutes; because it tends to raise the grain of the wood, the dulcimer is then sanded lightly, using 220-grade sandpaper on the flat surfaces and 000- or 0000-grade steel wool on the curved surfaces. One or two more coats of sanding sealer are applied; after each coat the dulcimer is again allowed to dry and sanded lightly as before. Finally, Homer sprays one heavy coat of full-strength lacquer—or two coats of thinned lacquer—over the entire dulcimer; this is the final coat and will dry in approximately one hour.

If linseed oil was used to protect the fingerboard before spraying, the coating of unwanted lacquer can be skimmed from the fingerboard with a chisel or a scraper blade; because of a reaction between the lacquer and the drier in the linseed oil, after four hours the lacquer will be sufficiently hardened to peel off. If masking tape was used to cover the fingerboard, the tape is removed and the surface of the fingerboard may now be treated with boiled linseed oil; Homer says that this oil produces a very fine, durable top surface for the fingerboard, becoming part of the wood and helping to prevent oil from the player's fingers from entering the wood. If humidity is high, it is best to allow linseed oil to stand overnight to harden.

Linseed or tung oil can also be used instead of lacquer to provide a fine overall dulcimer finish. The oil is applied to the surface of the wood and allowed to stand for approximately 30 minutes, after which the excess is wiped off. Depending upon the temperature and humidity, the dulcimer should then be set aside overnight or even for a couple of days until all the oil has soaked well into the wood. Finally, one of two procedures can be followed: at one-week intervals for the next three weeks, a coat of oil can be applied to the dulcimer; or a coat of paste wax may be applied immediately and the dulcimer polished to a wax shine. If the latter procedure is chosen, after a few weeks—when the dulcimer begins to look a bit dull—a thin film of oil may be applied to the surface and left overnight (at this stage not much oil will penetrate); the following morning, the surface should be very lightly scoured with 0000-grade steel wool, then waxed heavily and polished with a soft cloth. Thereafter, to restore the luster of the finish, all that is needed is to wax and polish it.

Some dulcimer craftsmen prefer an oil finish, believing that a better tone is thereby achieved; others believe that oil tends to load the wood—or make it heavier—and can therefore cause a slight deadening of sound. Homer prefers the lacquer finish; judging from the excellent tone of his dulcimers, his preference is more than justified.

36. Sawing off ends of back flush with end block

37. Using pocketknife to trim rough edges

INSTALLING STAPLE FRETS

After the instrument has acquired a satisfactory finish, the traditional staple-type frets, if they are to be used on the fingerboard, may be driven into place with a small, preferably plastic-headed, hammer; as already indicated, the holes for these frets were punched during the shaping of the fingerboard. (If mandolin or guitar frets were chosen, they were installed during the construction of the fingerboard.) The insertion of staple-type frets, as the last step in the unified body assembly, also serves as a testing device for the soundness of the dulcimer's construction, because they must be hammered into the fingerboard of the fully assembled instrument.

As a "stickler" for tradition, Homer does not approve of using guitar frets on a dulcimer; he believes "the little wire frets are best. . . . they are perfectly round, and when you drive them down in the fingerboard, they are just beautiful, and they don't wear out very fast. . . . and your strings will last a little longer; old time makers used to make their traditional staple frets out of brass safety pins." To make the staples, he uses one of two methods: if he is working on just one dulcimer, he may simply measure off and bend small pieces of wire, such as broom-maker's wire, with pliers, so that the ends are turned down like those of a staple; the ends are then driven into the holes in the fingerboard (fig. 38). More often, however—especially if he is working on several dulcimers—Homer uses his own homemade fretmaker, which both cuts the wire to exact length and bends the ends to the proper staple shape; Homer feeds wire into the fret maker and thus cuts and shapes several frets at the same time (fig. 39). Although any type of wire may be used, nickel, copper, or brass are perhaps best, as they are decorative and rust resistant. The frets may run completely across the fingerboard or only partly across, usually depending on the craftsman's preference; however, the oldest traditional dulcimers had staple frets only about half way across the width of the fingerboard, often under only one string.

After the frets are hammered in place, the fully assembled dulcimer body is then ready for the installation of its adjustable or movable parts—the pegs, the bridge, and the strings.

38. Driving staple-type frets into fingerboard

39. Using homemade fret-maker

STRINGING THE DULCIMER

One by one, each of the strings is pulled through the hole already drilled for it in the end block; the balled ends will catch in the notch, where they are held securely (fig. 16).

Next, the pegs are inserted into the pegbox. After aligning each string with its proper peg, Homer drills a 1/16-inch string hole in each peg with an electric hand drill (fig. 40); because an improperly placed string hole can cause the string to kick its peg out of the pegbox, the string holes should not be drilled until the pegs have been inserted and aligned. Once the holes are drilled, the bass string—the string farthest away from the player, or the bottom string if the dulcimer is held like a guitar—is carefully wound around the peg so that the string winds against the side of the pegbox. The peg should be turned forward, or clockwise, and the string should be wound over the top of the peg (fig. 41); otherwise it will tend to kick the peg out of the pegbox rather than hold it in. The screwlike action of the string winding in toward the inside surface of the pegbox actually holds the peg stable and prevents it from slipping.

All of the strings should be wound on their respective pegs in this manner. On a four-string dulcimer, the No. 2 string—the one next to the bass string—is wound on a peg on the same side as the bass peg; the No. 3 and No. 4 strings are then wound on the two pegs closest to the player (fig. 42). On a three-string dulcimer, the No. 2 and No. 3 strings are wound on the two pegs closest to the player, opposite the bass string peg (fig. 43). The pegs on the side closest to the player are also turned clockwise, and the string is wound over the top of the peg and in against the face of the pegbox. Even after following this procedure, however, the pegs may still slip, especially on hot, dry days when the wood dries out and contracts. Conversely, the peg that was loose in dry weather may expand and become tight in humid weather. Such variation is normal, and only if the peg consistently slips must it be treated (see page 101).

After winding the strings around their pegs but before drawing them tight, Homer slides the adjustable bridge into place about half an inch from the end block; the bridge is notched where the strings are to be pulled over it. The bridge on a Ledford dulcimer can be moved forward or backward to adjust the pitch of the scale according to the preference of the individual player. For example, a player may wish to tune the dulcimer to a key matching the range of his or her voice; if the dulcimer must be tuned either extremely high or extremely low to accomplish this, its intonation may be destroyed unless the bridge can be moved forward (to facilitate a high tuning) or backward (to facilitate a low tuning). Therefore, a portable or adjustable bridge—not glued in place but merely held stationary by the tension of the strings—allows a greater flexibility of tonal pitch. Homer's first dulcimers did not have movable bridges (fig. 17), but he quickly learned that his instruments became more flexible with them. However, during construction of the fingerboard, the normal position of the bridge—as previously indicated—should be marked so that if the bridge is accidentally knocked out of place, or all the strings are removed at one time and the bridge falls off, the player will know where it is normally positioned.

Once the bridge is put into place and the strings are tightened, the assembly of the dulcimer is completed; the instrument is ready to tune and play.

40 (*above*). Drilling holes in pegs for strings
41 (*below*). Proper method of stringing the dulcimer

42. Proper stringing
of 4-string dulcimer

43. Proper stringing
of 3-string dulcimer

A LEDFORD FOUR-STRING DULCIMER
IN C-MAJOR (IONIAN) TUNING

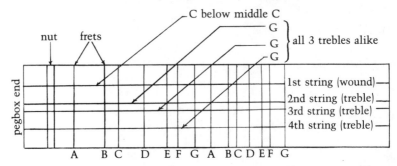

Note: The double (melody) string is in the middle. It can be moved to the outside for those who prefer to use wooden noters.

Ionian mode: C G G G

Mixolydian mode: D G G G

Aeolian (minor) mode: C G G B♭

TUNING THE DULCIMER

On the dulcimer a single string normally carries the melody, while the remaining strings are strummed as drone accompaniment. When the dulcimer is laid flat on a player's lap, with the tuning pegs to the player's left (the traditional position), then Homer numbers the strings, beginning with the one *farthest* from the player, 1-2-3, and 4, if it is a four-string dulcimer. (Homer says this is the proper way to identify strings; he does not follow the latter-day convention of numbering the strings from the player's side out.) Fret numbering starts with the fret closest to the pegs. If it is remembered that the frets on a dulcimer are placed so that they will correspond to the white keys on a piano, tuning a dulcimer is easily accomplished, and tunes may be picked out as readily as one plays tunes on white piano keys. (The accompanying diagram illustrates the following tuning information.)

To tune the dulcimer to the key of C in what is called the Ionian or major mode—the tuning preferred by most people—the first string is tuned to the piano's C below middle C, and the peg is secured to hold the string in tune at C. The second string is tuned to the piano's G below middle C (you can find this note by sounding the first string with your finger pressed just to the left side of the fourth fret); then the third and fourth strings are tuned to exactly the same G as the second. Therefore, starting with the No. 1 string, the notes should be C G G G (or C G G, if there are only three strings). "Amazing Grace" is played most often in this tuning. Homer says that because his scale is somewhat different from those of other dulcimers—his first fret is actually closer to the nut than most—the common tunings often produce a different sound on his instruments. He says that the more widespread standard scale on other dulcimers will often cause flats on one fret and sharps on another.

Tuning for the Mixolydian mode—often used for playing "Old Joe Clark"—is accomplished simply by changing *just* the bass (No. 1) string, tuning it one whole step up from C to D. Mixolydian tuning—D G G G, or D G G—Homer says, automatically makes the remaining G strings (which are not retuned) sound tonic.

Tuning to the Aeolian—or minor—mode on Homer's dulcimers is as easily accomplished as tuning for the Mixolydian because, again, only one string needs to be changed. Starting with the major or Ionian tuning (C G G G or C G G), the string closest to the player is changed from G to B-flat. To do this, Homer simply puts his finger on the first fret of that last string and tunes it so that it sounds C— like the first string—when pressed; thus when it is "open" (not pressed down), it will sound B-flat. This puts the strings in the Aeolian mode: C G G B-flat or C G B-flat. Tunes commonly played in this mode are "Pretty Polly," "Greensleeves," and (one of Homer's favorites) "I'm Just Going Over Jordan."

PERSONALIZING YOUR DULCIMER

Various methods can be used to individualize a dulcimer. Mother-of-pearl initials or names can be inlaid in several areas: the side of the scrolled pegbox, the fingerboard, the middle of the back. In general, however, Homer believes that dulcimer sides should not be ornamented; he prefers to construct them of solid but particularly beautiful wood, such as curly walnut, curly cherry, or curly maple, even though using figured woods for dulcimer sides requires the craftsman to heat or steam the side strip before inserting it into the dulcimer body. Mother-of-pearl can also be used in less personal but still decorative fashion; it can be cut into the shape of a star, a crown, a fleur-de-lis, or a simple circle. When used as position markers on the fingerboard, the pearl pieces may be cut into shape notes; for example, C (do) can be designated by a triangle; E (mi) by a diamond, and so on. If desired, the owner's initials can be engraved into the pearl. In place of pearl, holly tree wood may used for inlays.

Scrollwork and decorative shading can be achieved through wood-burning; however, this process reduces or lowers the surface of the wood and must not be used over a wide area or in delicate components such as the sides. The pegbox is the ideal place for woodburning ornamentation.

Homer cautions that decoration of dulcimer tops—except for the fingerboard—should be limited to the shaping of sound holes; sound holes can be cut in the shape of a heart, a diamond, a club, a fleur-de-lis, a circle, a scroll, a shape note, or just about any design small enough to suit the limited area of the dulcimer top. When shaping ornate sound holes, however, the craftsman must avoid creating small, jutting pieces of wood that will break at a finger's pressure—unless, or course, he is willing somehow to reinforce that area on the underside of the top.

THE TWO-PIECE INLAID BACK

Homer uses the following method to create the especially beautiful two-piece inlaid back for his dulcimer. After a board that is normally used to make a dulcimer back has been smoothed down on both sides with the jointer and its surfaces have been at least rough-sanded, the table saw is used to rip the board down to a bit more than half the width of the back of the dulcimer—approximately 3 5/8 inches. The table saw is further used to slab off a piece of wood about 1/8 inch thick from each side of the board. Then one of these two pieces is turned over and placed next to the second; the grains of the two pieces of wood should now match and form a pattern; this process is called "book matching" and will produce a beautiful design, especially if figured—that is, burl, curly, or crotch—walnut is used.

Homer then carefully aligns the two pieces of wood that will form the back, seeing that they match and that the edges are flush, and glues them together with aliphatic glue. To ensure a solid joint between the two pieces, pressure must be applied to hold them together while the glue is drying. However, the pieces are so thin that under the pressure necessary for a good glue joint, and with no other support, they would buckle or bend; and clamps cannot be used to apply the needed pressure against the bare wood, as they would mar the surface.

Until just recently, Homer experienced considerable difficulty in joining the two-piece back because of its tendency to bend or buckle; he used various makeshift methods to apply pressure simultaneously to the sides of the glued halves (to form a strong joint) and to the top of the back (to prevent the thin wood from buckling). A simple and temporary plywood frame enabled him to apply lateral pressure, but he still had to stack weights on top the two-piece back to prevent it from buckling at the glued jointure. He used concrete blocks, metal mill-end pieces, or any heavy material at hand that would fit in the restricted area of the frame.

Because Homer had always been dissatisfied with such a make-shift, he recently invented an ingenious new frame-and-press combination, designed for the specific needs of his two-piece back construction process. The adjustable frame not only permits different sizes of backs to be placed in it and holds the pieces together while the glue dries but also prevents the back from buckling under the lateral pressure (fig. 44). The cranks used to tighten the horizontal pressure are made from large nails, bent to form handles that can be turned like cranks. Vertical pressure is achieved by several swinging pieces of wood that can be swiveled to apply more or less pressure as needed to the top of the back, thus allowing the boards to remain perfectly flat and under tension while the glued halves dry to form a solid, matched two-piece back.

After the glue is dry, the back is removed from its frame, and Homer scrapes the glue off both sides with a cabinet scraper until there is a smooth surface at the joint. The cabinet scraper, which has two handles and a blade mounted at a sharp angle, can be used to skim off the glue without digging into the wood. Then on the inside surface of the back, the glued joint is reinforced with a 1/2- inch-wide, 1/8- inch-thick strip of plywood, or other very thin wood, which runs the entire length of the jointure; the length of the strip can be cut to exact dimension after it has been glued onto the dulcimer back. The grain of the reinforcement strip must run at right angles to that of the back; if the grain runs the same way, it will provide little reinforcement and, under stress, will likely split along with the joint. Both edges of the reinforcement strip should be beveled. Using aliphatic glue, Homer positions this reinforcement strip and, after placing a protective piece of wood between the back and the clamp to prevent marring, clamps it with C-clamps along the full inside length of the back; weights may be laid atop it, but because aliphatic glue is being used, not much pressure is needed. It is then allowed to dry for thirty minutes before removing the clamps.

The two-piece back is now ready to be inlaid. Using a table saw, Homer cuts a groove along the outside of the dulcimer back, directly down the middle of the joint. Thus, a part of the joint is actually cut out to make room for the inlay; in fact, the cut is usually made all the way through the back and even about halfway through the thickness of the reinforcement strip, or roughly the depth of the thickness of the strip to be inlaid. The width of the cut is, of course, determined by the width of the inlay strip but probably should be no more than 3/16 inch to avoid an "over-inlaid" look. A specially ground-down dado blade, which cuts the exact width needed, facilitates this process. To cut the groove, Homer adjusts the fence of the table saw so that the blade falls directly in the middle of the joint; the outside edges of this dulcimer back, it must be remembered, have not yet been shaped to the dulcimer contours, so the sides of the board

44. Homemade press for making 2-piece back

are straight and parallel with the center joint. Homer then runs the back through the saw, holding the wood firmly against the saw table so that the groove will be of equal depth all along the length of the back.

After the slot is cut, aliphatic glue is carefully squeezed into it, and then one end of the inlay strip is laid into the groove. This may be a marquetry strip, purchased from a commercial source, or a homemade strip of white holly, maple, or other contrasting wood. Homer then drives the inlay strip into the groove with a small plastic-headed hammer (fig. 45); after the glue dries, he scrapes off the excess with a cabinet scraper and sands the strip area, using a flat sanding block and either 100- or 150-grade sandpaper. The two-piece inlaid back is now ready to be shaped and assembled as part of a dulcimer (fig. 46).

45. Tapping inlay in place in 2-piece back

46. Book-matched dulcimer back, with inlay

MOTHER-OF-PEARL INLAYING

If using rough-shell pearl, the first step in inlaying is to cut the rough shell, using a metal-cutting band saw, into whatever size chunks are needed and then to grind those pieces flat on a carbide steel wheel (mother-of-pearl can, if you prefer, be bought already ground flat). The steel wheel, with carbide embedded in its sides, is available commercially and can be used on the table saw or can itself be mounted on a motor. A diamond wheel can be used instead, but Homer believes that it tends to waste the pearl, whereas the carbide wheel conserves the material and accomplishes the task more quickly. The pearl is ground wet; it is necessary to have a pan of water nearby so that it can be kept wet at all times. Because pearl dust is highly toxic, Homer always wears a respirator while grinding it; the craftsman must be extremely careful not to inhale the dust from mother-of-pearl at any time.

After the pieces are ground flat, they may be cut into designs. To support the pearl while cutting and to help prevent breaking, Homer uses the following procedure: a board approximately one inch wide, 1/2 inch thick, and seven or eight inches long is clamped to the workbench. Next, a 1/4-inch-diameter hole is drilled about an inch from one end of the board, and a slot is cut with a band saw from that end of the board to the hole. A piece of pearl is placed on top of this board, covering the drilled hole; the pearl should have either the desired design drawn on it or a paper design glued to it. A jeweler's saw with a No. 3 blade is inserted into the slot in the end of the piece of wood, and the mother-of-pearl is brought up to it; by allowing the blade of the saw to work up and down in the 1/4-inch hole, Homer can cut the pearl to the exact shape of the design (fig. 47). The saw is always pulled toward the handle, and it is essential that the blade be inserted in the saw so that the teeth are pointed downward toward the handle; otherwise, the saw blade and sometimes the pearl piece will break. When the piece of pearl has been cut to as nearly perfect a shape as possible with the saw, it is removed from the support board and—with needle files, flat files, or regular rattail files—filed to exact shape and dimension. (The respirator should be used during filing, and at all times when pearl dust is present.) The pearl is then ready for inlaying.

Numerous areas on a dulcimer can be attractively decorated with pearl inlays, one obvious surface being the fingerboard, which will be discussed here by way of example. Four inlays are typically used on the dulcimer fingerboard, one each at notes C (between the second and third frets), E (between the fourth and fifth frets), G (between the sixth and seventh frets), and high C (between the ninth and tenth frets).

To begin the inlay process, the fingerboard is first covered with masking tape, and the pearl is laid down on the tape, making certain that the piece is in the exact position wanted for the inlay. For an inlay between frets, the piece is centered on the fingerboard halfway between the two frets. Next, a very sharp-pointed knife is used to cut around the piece of pearl and through the tape; then the pearl is removed and the little piece of tape that has been cut loose is pulled away from the fingerboard, leaving a hole in the tape that perfectly matches the shape of the pearl (fig. 48). Homer repeats this process for each pearl inlay.

Various tools can be used to cut the inlay holes in the fingerboard itself: pocketknife, for example, or a pocketknife in conjunction with a chisel; however, both of these methods are slow and painstaking, the latter being only a little less time consuming. Because he says that it is more efficient, at least for the initial cutting, Homer recommends using a Dremel high-speed grinder with a router bit; if desired, a chisel can be used later to finish shaping the hole. If the router is used initially, the craftsman should first cut around the outline of the hole with a small—size 1/16—bit, being careful not to touch the masking tape, or the hole will be too large for the inlay; the tape is a perfect guide because it can always be seen. After the initial cutting, an even smaller drill—Homer has himself designed and made a size 3/64—can be used to "chew" out the hole. The drill is repeatedly pushed in and pulled out, pushed in and pulled out, traveling in an up-and-down rather than a side-to-side motion and making a sort of hole in a hole in a hole. The craftsman must have an extremely steady hand to do this. An expert like Homer can drill the hole so exactly to the size of the pearl piece that all he will have to do is drop the inlay into the hole and, with a piece of flat steel push it into place. Glue will not even be necessary. However, less skillful craftsmen can rout a hole larger than the pearl piece, put the pearl in place, and then fill around it.

When finished, the hole should be flat-bottomed and deep enough so that the inlay, when inserted in the hole, lies level with the surface of the fingerboard; if the piece juts above the surface, smoothing it down will be a tedious and time-consuming job. Therefore, it is essential to hollow out the hole to a depth that exactly equals the thickness of the pearl plus any glue needed to secure it.

If glue is necessary, various types may be used; Elmer's Glue-All, Weldwood plastic resin, clear plastic cement, or the new aliphatic glues all qualify. If the cement is used, two coats must be applied, allowing thirty minutes for the first to dry before the second can be applied. Weldwood glue also takes time to dry—approximatley four hours—but it dries extremely hard, like concrete, and will not shrink; for these reasons it is probably superior to other glues, or at least as good as aliphatic, for pearl. Homer suggests that an excellent paste can be made in which to set mother-of-pearl by mixing water with Weldwood glue and adding fine sawdust from the wood that is being inlaid; such a mixture forms an extra thick paste, much thicker than would normally be used for a glue joint.

After the glue is put into the hole, the pearl is pressed in with a flat steel tool such as a file or a discarded jointer blade. The surface of the pearl must be completely covered by the surface of the tool used to press it in place; if the pressure is not equal, the pearl piece may break.

The inlay will probably fit tightly into the hole and even bind to some extent—indeed, it must, or it is likely later to fall out. The pearl piece must be pressed all the way to the bottom of the hole; when it is securely in place and level with the top of the wood, the excess glue must be washed off and the inlay allowed to dry.

If the pearl is inlaid in the fingerboard before the frets go in, the entire fingerboard—inlays included—can be smoothed at one time. Either a file or a flat block with sandpaper wrapped around it —150-grade for the first sanding and 220-grade for the second—will dress down the fingerboard nicely. To make the mother-of-pearl inlay even shinier, 260-grade sandpaper or a buffer may be used on it.

For an additional ornamental touch, small lines may be cut into the pearl with an engraver and the surface painted with a thin film of black lacquer or India ink and allowed to dry; then the excess lacquer (or ink) on the surface of the pearl is sanded off. The lacquer (or ink) remaining in the little engraved lines will produce a decorative appearance (figs. 49 and 50). Homer says that such engraving is difficult, however, as pearl does not have a constant or stable texture as does, say, brass; pearl is alternately hard, then soft, and it chips easily, causing the craftsman—if he is not careful—to lose control of his engraving tool. As Homer describes it: "You've started around some of those nice little curves and you think you've got it made, and all of a sudden [the engraver] slips all the way across, skips some place else, and makes three or four more grooves than you wanted." Pearl inlays can also be etched with acid or with diamond-tipped gravure tools, but Homer believes that hand engraving, although it can be difficult to control, is probably preferable.

Mother-of-pearl can be attractively inlaid in the back or sides of the pegbox as well as the fingerboard. Also, in a book-matched inlaid dulcimer back, mother-of-pearl can be used in combination with marquetry or strip inlays; for example, a pearl design can be placed in the center of the wood inlay, or perhaps three pearl designs can be spaced equally along its length for a more variegated appearance. In whatever way it is used, mother-of-pearl indeed provides an attractive addition to the dulcimer, and Homer is adept at decorating his instruments with pearl inlays.

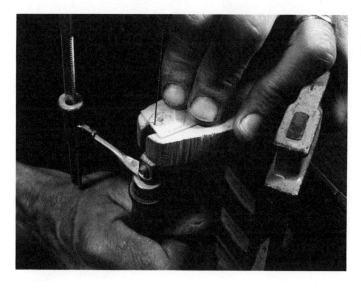

47. Sawing pearl design

48 (*above*). Masking for mother-of-pearl inlay; 49 (*below*). Inlaid mother-of-pearl

50. Inlaid
mother-of-pearl

ADJUSTMENTS AND REPAIRS

Pegs. After long use, dulcimer pegs may become glazed and slick, thus losing their "bite" or friction. Unless the player pushes the pegs in exceptionally hard while turning them, such pegs will slip during tuning. To correct the condition, the string should be removed from the peg and the peg from the pegbox; the peg should then be turned one time—one complete revolution, no more—in a piece of 100-grade sandpaper, taking off *just* enough wood to remove the gloss and roughen the surface so that the peg will hold. Homer warns that one should never sand only one side of a peg, or scrape it with a pocketknife; this would distort the roundness and taper, and prevent the peg from fitting properly in the pegbox.

A peg can also be made to hold more securely through the use of violin resin; it may be reduced to powder form by scraping the cake with a pocketknife, and the powder rubbed on the peg. When the peg is replaced in its hole, the powder should create enough friction to keep the peg from slipping. The disadvantage to this method is that the peg, when turned, will pop and squeak.

Homer, in jest, often cites an easier, though more destructive, method by which to prevent a peg from slipping: "As the old fiddler used to say, 'Take the peg out and spit on it and put it back in and make it stay put.' However, such a practice will in time be disastrous, as the peg hole and the peg itself will eventually be ruined."

If a dulcimer owner is unable to repair a peg so that it will not slip, he should return the instrument to its maker for repair. It is also important to make certain that the string is properly wound; if not, a peg may have sufficient friction but still slip (see pages 86-87 for instructions on winding a string).

Replacing Strings. Strings should be replaced on a dulcimer at least once every three months, whether or not the instrument is being played. If the dulcimer is played daily, the strings may need changing more often, especially if they are not wiped clean after each playing session; fingers deposit salt upon the strings, and if not removed, the salt will cause the strings to rust more quickly. Generally, a string begins to deteriorate the moment it is stretched across the fingerboard; long before it has rusted sufficiently to break, it will lose much of its flexibility and will produce sharp, or sometimes even flat, notes.

Standard-gauge guitar strings are suitable for dulcimers: for the bass string a G, or third (gauge .025), wound guitar string is recommended; the remaining strings may be trebles (gauge .012). It is best to use strings that already have balls at one end rather than the loop-end type; the loops require nails, small pins, or wire to keep them from pulling through the holes in the end block. It is possible to buy strings commercially packaged for dulcimers; however, these are merely guitar or banjo strings put in special packets. Homer uses strings manufactured under his own brand name and especially customized for the dulcimer; he also sells these strings by the package.

Fine Tuners. Homer says that if the owner so desires, the dulcimer can be fitted with fine tuners. Specifically designed for use with the violin and other stringed instruments, these devices provide the player with a graduated and controlled method by which to stretch and release the strings and thereby raise or lower their pitch with greater accuracy than can be accomplished with pegs alone.

Various types are available: one style—the same as that used on violin strings—simply clips onto the strings between the bridge and the end block (fig. 51). It requires a space of at least 1 1/4 inches; normally, the size of the dulcimer need not be altered to accommodate this tuner.

A second type is mounted in the end of the dulcimer's end block; it requires that the block be made longer than usual, thus lengthening the entire instrument. This tuner—the type that is used on the violin tailpiece—is mounted on a piece of metal (brass, stainless steel,

51. Fine tuners

or aluminum) and the metal piece is fastened down into the end block. The top of the block must be cut back at a 30° slant so that the tuner will be below the level of the strings where they cross the bridge.

A third method of fine tuning used by some dulcimer makers involves attaching guitar gears to the pegbox. Even though such gears do a fine job of tuning, Homer believes that they look incongruous on a traditionally designed dulcimer.

Frets. If a dulcimer is habitually exposed to marked changes in humidity, the fingerboard and the traditional staple-type frets may be adversely affected. Homer says that this is especially true of fingerboards made from soft woods—such as butternut—as they will expand and contract more readily than fingerboards constructed of harder woods such as black walnut (since Homer's dulcimers usually have black walnut fingerboards, this is not a frequent problem with the Ledford dulcimer). As the fingerboard expands and contracts with changes in moisture content, the staple frets—which are supported only at the ends, where they are driven into the wood—tend to bow up, causing the strings to buzz against them. To correct this problem, the strings must first be removed; then the frets can be tapped back down with a small, preferably plastic-headed, hammer until they are again level with the fingerboard.

Repairing a Dulcimer Body. Homer says that most body repairs are necessitated either by a split back or top, or by a side which has split or slipped out of place.

If the top, back, or side of a dulcimer is split, and if the crack is a clean break, it can often be repaired quite satisfactorily with aliphatic glue. Cracks running straight up and down through the thickness of the dulcimer top, back, or side are easiest to mend because they can be clamped while the glue is drying. However, if the wood splinters—that is, breaks so that it separates at a diagonal—the repair is quite difficult, if not impossible, to hold with clamps, so Homer recommends the following method.

With a fretsaw or a hacksaw, a slot is made at right angles to the surface of the dulcimer which is split. The slot should be the width of the thickness of the blade. If a wider slot is desired, a thin file or emory board can be used to file back both sides. Into this slot is fitted a spline—a piece of wood of the same kind and thickness as the dulcimer wood—which has been cut at a very slight angle and is slightly tapered or wedge shaped. The spline is firmly pressed into the slot with glue. It is important that the surface of the spline be level with the surface of the dulcimer, or an offset will occur. Because of its wedge shape, the spline should fit tightly into the slot; indeed, if it does not fit snugly, the spline will not stay glued and will fall out. After the glue has dried, the area can then be sanded and finished, and the repair is complete.

Another type of break that is often difficult to repair is one that runs across the grain of a dulcimer top or back. If the split is a clean break and all pieces can be fit back together, it is possible to force glue gently into the crack with a finger and, while pressing down on the area of the break, to crisscross the dulcimer with nylon tape, pulling it snug until it holds the sides of the crack firmly together while the glue dries. To reinforce the glued joint, it is necessary to pop out the dulcimer side; then, a spline or reinforcement strip must be glued on the inner surface of the cracked top or back, making certain that the grain of the spline runs crosswise to the break. This brace will neither destroy nor in any way alter the tone of the dulcimer; seemingly, if a dulcimer has been originally constructed to possess a tone of high quality, later reinforcement pieces have little or no effect upon that tone.

It is also possible for a side simply to become separated from the top or back. In such instances, repair is accomplished by inserting into the opening or crack a steel nail file or an emory board and carefully filing away the old glue. Then one can force new aliphatic glue into the joint and, with nylon tape, pull the side and its top or back tightly together. Homer says that it is important to wash off all excess glue, especially from the bare wood; although glue usually will not seriously harm the dulcimer finish, it is best to wipe off as much of the excess as posible before it dries in order to maintain a smooth, attractive finish.

In place of nylon tape, leather-lined spool-type clamps—called violin maker's clamps—can be used to hold the side and top or back together. To make his own version of these clamps—the same ones he uses in the dulcimer assembly—Homer follows this procedure: a broom handle is cut into one-inch sections; holes are drilled into the center of each section; and a 1/4-inch bolt is inserted through each hole. A washer and then a wing nut are added on the bolt that allows the clamps to be turned easily and quickly by hand (see the sketch on page 51). To protect the wood surface of the dulcimer, the clamps are lined with almost any type of leather (except perhaps an extremely soft variety such as glove leather); the leather from the upper part of a man's shoe is particularly good. When these clamps are used to hold a dulcimer top and bottom to a side, the bolt is vertical to the surface of the dulcimer so that it pulls the edges of the top and the back toward each other (fig. 34).

Occasionally a dulcimer peg may break, in which case a new one should be constructed, ideally by the original craftsman or another dulcimer maker. Homer warns that the main problem for the novice who tries to replace a peg would occur if he reamed out the peg hole again, thereby destroying the standard hole size; the peg would then have to be custom fit, a process entailing much long and tedious work.

The Dulcimer Finish. Most duclimer makers use natural finishes—preferably lacquers—which do not color the wood; therefore, it is a relatively simple operation to refinish an area that has been marred. If the wood has been stained, it is much more difficult to match the color should the finish become damaged.

To repair a scratch on a lacquered finish, Homer suggests merely touching the spot with a small artist's brush dipped in lacquer thinner. A scratch on a lacquered surface will always turn white, and it will disappear almost immediately when the thinner is applied. In most cases this treatment is sufficient to hide the scratch; however, if one wants to refinish the scratched area completely, he should first apply the thinner and then a spray or brushing lacquer. When the lacquer is dry, the area should be rubbed with a 220-grade sandpaper until it is level; then more lacquer, as many coats as desired, can be applied.

Only when the wood is badly bruised or cracked is it necessary to strip off the old finish. To do so, the surface is rubbed down with 000- or 0000-grade steel wool that has been dipped into lacquer thinner. This is a messy job which, Homer advises, should be done in an open place away from flames or fire, as fumes from lacquer thinner are similar to those of gasoline—they drift and can intoxicate or cause an explosion. Zip Strip varnish remover can also be used to get rid of the old finish. The remover is merely laid on with a brush; it is important *not* to brush back and forth over the surface; rather, the remover should be applied with one brush motion and allowed to stand for at least thirty minutes. Then either steel wool or an old cloth, or even sawdust or wood shavings from the jointer, can be used to wipe off the old finish. If the area needing attention is relatively small, not requiring the use of varnish remover, removal of the old finish can be accomplished with a scraper blade—using extreme care, of course, not to bite into the wood. After the old finish is removed and, if need be, the dulcimer repaired, the area can be sprayed with the same type of finish as was originally used.

To eradicate a surface mar in a dulcimer with an oil finish, one should first rub the area with fine 000- or 0000-grade steel wool, being careful to rub *with* the grain, not across it. Next, boiled linseed or tung oil should be applied and left on for a day or two; then the dulcimer can be rewaxed and polished.

SECURING THE DULCIMER FOR PLAYING

Because the dulcimer is a lightweight, smoothly finished instrument, it is necessary to devise some method to avoid its slipping around on, or off, the player's lap during performance. Here are a few of Homer's suggestions.

If the dulcimer, like Homer's, has an overhanging top and back— that is, the top and back overlap the sides—a bent paper clip may be fastened on each end of the instrument, over the edge of the overhanging back. To protect the finish of the dulcimer, double-faced rug tape may be used to cover the areas where the clips will fasten. Then rubber bands can be stretched across the back of the dulcimer between the paper clips; the rubber bands will cling to the fabric of the player's dress or pants and keep the dulcimer from sliding (fig. 52). The same effect can be achieved by sticking two small pieces or one strip of double-faced rug tape at each end of the dulcimer back. The tape will not permanently harm the finish of the dulcimer, but it will leave a sticky residue that must be removed with either rubbing alcohol or mild detergent.

Another possibility is to build a small table or stand—an ironing-board-like affair—to hold the dulcimer stationary. To make it more portable, Homer's stand has folding legs. Supporting brackets on the ends allow the dulcimer to fit down into the stand, which has been hollowed out and lined with felt. The dulcimer then rests on felt at either end and is completely suspended in the middle (fig. 53). Not only does this stand hold the instrument stable for playing, but it also adds to the dulcimer's volume without destroying any of its characteristic sweetness of tone.

Other methods may be used to hold the dulcimer stationary: a guitar strap that fastens on each end of the dulcimer and encircles the player's back; or rubber commode-seat bumpers fastened on the back of the dulcimer, one on the pegbox end and two on the end block end, which enable it to sit solidly on a table.

52. Use of rubber bands to secure dulcimer on lap

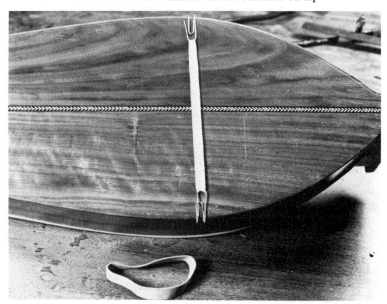

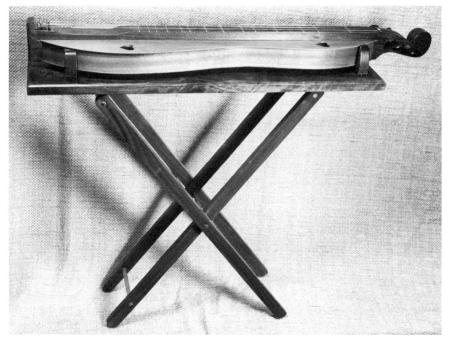

53. Homer's homemade dulcimer stand

CLEANING AND STORING

Homer suggests that one of the best places in a home to store a dulcimer is on top of a piano or, if it does not become too hot, on top of the television or stereo. In such a position, not only is the dulcimer decorative and convenient, but the vibration of the piano— or television or stereo—causes the dulcimer itself to vibrate and thus eventually improves the tonal quality of the instrument. Homer sometimes makes special brackets to suspend the dulcimer so that its top and back are visible, rather than the sides.

A dulcimer can also be hung on a wall, preferably an inside partition; an outside wall may emit moisture, which would damage the back of the instrument unless small pads are placed behind the dulcimer to prevent direct contact. Homer warns that because of the danger of damage from moisture, the dulcimer should not be placed near an open window. If a dulcimer does become damp, the best remedy is time; the instrument should be left in a place where humidity is temperate, and it will dry out by itself. One should not attempt to dry the dulcimer near a fire, or other heat source, as abrupt changes in moisture may crack the thin wood. If the dulcimer becomes so damp that the pegs swell and will not turn, it is best to put the instrument aside without playing it; in no case should the pegs be forced. If they *must* be loosened immediately, set a block of wood on the small end of a peg and tap the block gently with a hammer—using a sharp, quick blow—and the peg should loosen.

In general, Homer believes that if a dulcimer has been well constructed and finely finished, normal exposure to atmospheric moisture will do little harm. On the contrary, he says, dryness is a more destructive enemy; therefore, a dulcimer should never be set or hung near a vent or any other source from which hot air is blowing. Hot air dries wood out excessively, causing it to crack, or to separate at the joints. In fact, it is best to store the dulcimer away from any flow of air; especially beware of placing it near a heating duct or an air conditioning vent. Nor should the dulcimer be left in direct sunlight, as rays from the sun will bleach the wood and dry it out.

A dulcimer can be safely kept in a specially built case, if the case is periodically opened to air out. Homer often makes dulcimer cases (fig. 54) on special order, and he advises that to control the moisture accumulating in a dulcimer case, silica gel or some other moisture-absorbing substance should be kept in the case at all times.

54. Homer's homemade dulcimer case

Homer warns that extremes in temperature, as well as in humidity, can also be damaging to a dulcimer. For example, if an instrument has been left in a car during bitterly cold winter weather and has become thoroughly chilled, it would be unwise immediately to expose the dulcimer to the 70° or 72° temperature of a heated house; such an abrupt change might split the wood, separate the instrument at its joints, or at least crack its finish. To prevent such damage, the dulcimer must be warmed up slowly: it may be left in a case or wrapped in a towel or cloth for about an hour.

To clean a dulcimer, the surface should be wiped carefully with a soft cotton cloth. If the surface is slightly soiled, it can be wiped with a damp cloth and—if necessary—a small amount of mild household detergent, after which the surface should be immediately wiped dry. As the dulcimer finish is fairly durable and reasonably impervious to dirt, it will seldom become badly soiled; usually, dusting will suffice.

Following Homer's suggestions for storing, cleaning, and providing loving care for the traditional Appalachian dulcimer should enable any owner to enjoy this remarkable instrument to the fullest for many years.

III

THE LEDFORD DULCIMER IN CONTEXT

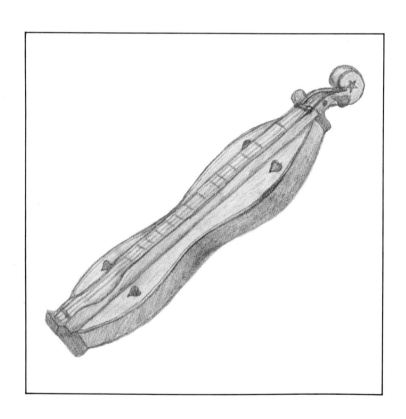

Homer and his dulcimer craft are inextricably grounded in and bounded by the sociocultural, psychological, socioeconomic, and political milieu of American society. Thus it is impossible, from a scholarly perspective, fully to appreciate the origins and the evolution of the Ledford dulcimer without first acquiring some understanding of the cultural contexts, or systems, in which we as Americans live.

Operating within our modern industrialized society are three systems of culture identified by various scholars as folk culture, popular culture, and elite culture.[1] All three systems have influenced and continue to influence Homer's craft in various ways, although the influences of folk and elite cultures probably have been more noticeable than those of popular culture. In order to appreciate and understand the contribution of each of these categories to Homer Ledford's development as a craftsman and consequently to his dulcimer craft, a brief discussion of the nature of culture, as well as a brief delineation of the three systems is essential.

In essence, culture is everything that a human being is, does, and creates beyond the biophysiological aspects of being a human being; however, the manner in which we attend to biophysiological processes is also cultural. Culture is essentially a process, or a mode, or a system, both of acquiring knowledge or learning and of demonstrating or expressing that knowledge and learning—the values, attitudes, mores, tendencies, preferences, proclivities, beliefs, sophistications, and so on that govern one's life. This conception of culture is particularly crucial to an understanding of folk culture, as folk culture—and by extension folklore—has for too long been defined primarily in terms of group. It is true, of course, that the people who are integral to the folk cultural process may constitute a group, but to define folk culture—or folklore—by utilizing group as part of the defintion is both erroneous and misleading. This is not to say, of course, that groups—formed for whatever reason—have no folkore; *all* groups "possess" folklore or, rather, have folk culture contributing to their overall makeup; likewise, all *people* "have" folk culture contributing to their complex identities, but one person may belong to several groups in today's complex society, thus complicating matters for the observer or analyst. To be more exact, people actually do not "have" or "possess" "culture;" rather, all people, and every group, learn and retain knowledge and share, express, and perpetuate it in what we see as three basic manners or systems—processes—that we call folk, popular, and elite culture; and the sociocultural essence of all people and all groups is composed of an intricate complex of all three systems.

In delineating the differences between folk, popular, and elite cultural processes or modes, it is essential first to understand that no one system is exclusive of any other; rather, in our modern complex society, there is constant integration of cultural modes. Consequently, as indicated earlier, a boundary cannot be drawn around a group of people in an attempt to identify that group as folk, popular, or elite; however, it is possible to state that a groups' activities or products reflect at any given time predominantly either elite, popular, or folk culture. However, such analysis must be made for each group phenomenon each time it occurs or exists, as various changes can alter the cultural nature of a phenomenon. It must be further remembered that no group today manifests only one set of cultural characteristics exclusively; for example, a coliseum concert by a bluegrass band (predominantly popular culture) will reflect many folk characteristics both in musical compositions and playing style, yet the performers might have learned music via formal music instruction (elite culture), and certainly the knowledge of how to construct most of the instruments they play is elite cultural knowledge. No group in modern complex society is enclaved or sheltered to such an extent that its cultural dimensions are exclusively those of any *one* of the cultural systems; rather each group will reflect aspects of all three cultural systems to some degree, although usually one cultural system will be predominant.

The same is also true for individuals. Indeed, the entire cultural dimension of even one individual, such as Homer, existing as he does in our modern complex society, necessarily comprises all three cultural processes. A given individual—say, by virtue of his occupation—may be considered predominantly an adherent of either elite, popular, or folk culture; at the same time, the other two systems will, to a considerable degree, also contribute to that individual's overall sociocultural identity. For example, Homer, by virtue of his occupation as a dulcimer maker and his heritage as a folk craftsman, without doubt is seen as a folk-culture-oriented individual. Yet he sometimes uses aspects of popular culture to market his dulcimers, and certainly mass tastes and interests have affected his craft. Homer and his craft have been affected by elite culture, too, especially via his institutionalized training in industrial arts. Only by examining a specific sociocultural phenomenon in terms of its origins, past influences, and contemporary contexts can one determine at any given point in time and place whether that phenomenon is predominantly folk, popular, or elite. With these reservations, then, a delineation of the characteristics of the three modes or processes of culture present in modern society follows.[2]

The system of popular culture is predominant in our society; it is the most widespread and the most adhered to by the majority of people. Elite and folk culture are less pervasive systems. The continuing dominance of popular culture in our society is probably assured because its channels of transmission are the all-pervasive and perennially popular mass media: television, radio, newspapers, magazines, motion pictures, mass marketing, and so on. Popular culture is created primarily by commercial interests—advertising people, A&R (artists and repertoire) people, journalists, business people, and such—for the primary purpose of making money as quickly and on as large a scale as possible; consequently, popular culture is directed toward the anonymous, heterogeneous majority, the masses, the "consumers" of our society; it is designed to prompt people to accept and buy various commercial products: cosmetics, clothing styles, records, soaps and so on.

In contrast, the elite cultural system is created and perpetuated by the so-called intelligentsia: the academicians, the politicians, the "experts" and scholars of the various learned disciplines. Elite cultural processes are usually transmitted via formal, institutionalized, professional, and educational programs and are directed to an individualistic, heterogeneous minority, which nevertheless can be very much a clique and even worldwide in scope. Elite culture is designed both to perpetuate the "tried and true" and to provide opportunity to create anew, to make new discoveries, in whatever field. Not only does elite culture retain and perpetuate its traditional knowledge but a primary purpose of elite culture is to evoke a personal response in its devotees and often to shock them into new awarenesses, new perceptions, ideas, realizations; therefore, progress is often the key word, demanding a constant search for new knowledge.

Although it may sound trite, folk culture nonetheless is probably best described by paraphrasing Abraham Lincoln: it is a culture of the people, by the people, and for the people; it is, to use another hackneyed phrase, grass-roots culture. The system of folk culture is created and perpetuated by the people themselves and transmitted from individual to individual via social situations that are relatively informal, unorganized, personal, intimate, usually noncommercial, and nonofficial; often the folk cultural mode of communication is that of imitation. Folk cultural knowledge, processes, or modes are absorbed by a sort of sociocultural osmosis afforded by a personal intimacy, over a relatively long period of time, between the receiver of the culture and people who already express it. Major purposes of folk culture are to teach models for living and to express humanity at society's relatively informal, unofficial level.

A brief illustration of these three systems of culture operating simultaneously but more or less independently can be found in cookery. Mass-media-provided recipes (in magazines, in newspapers, on boxes and cans of food products) and health hints (for example, margarine and vegetable oil advertisements) are products of popular culture. Home economics or cooking classes in academic or institutionalized settings and diets provided by medical doctors are illustrations of elite cultural processes. Folk culture includes everything not learned about cookery from popular and elite culture—that is, the knowledge about foods and cooking and eating that one acquires from family and friends. In essence, folk culture constitutes all that one learns *other than* from classrooms, museums, journals, textbooks and the like (elite culture processes), *other than* from mass media—radio, TV, movies, comics, rock concerts, newspapers, and the like (popular culture sources).

It should be understood, however, that it is possible to communicate elite knowledge via mass media, public educational television being a prime example. Yet it is *not* possible to communicate folk culture via mass media; folk culture performances or demonstrations of knowledge require natural contexts, and the artificial contexts of mass media inhibit, distort, and often even destroy the very nature of the folk cultural process. I am fond of saying that folk cultural communication requires at least two warm bodies, not one warm body and one warm tube. If a folk singer's performance is broadcast on television, the most one can say is that it is a media *representation* of a folk-culture performance. (This is not to say, on the other hand, that information garnered from either elite or popular cultural presentations cannot be adopted and adapted by the folk cultural process; parodies of all kinds exemplify such adoptions and adaptations.)

Likewise, it is impossible to capture most forms of folk culture in other media; it is impossible to have, for example, a folktale "in" literature. Folktales are more than just words; they are, as Robert Georges has discerned, folk cultural "storytelling events."[3] To share in that event, one needs to be personally present when the tale is told, so that one not only hears the words but also appreciates and comprehends how the words are used, where, when, by whom, to and for whom, and why they are used. One needs to experience the communal effect of the live communicative process; *that* is a folktale; that is folk culture, in context and in process. Any literary scholar will be quick to admit that not even dialect can be represented accurately in print; moreover, print cannot possibly convey intonation, modulation, timbre, nuance: the paralinguistic and nonverbal dimensions of what we call storytelling. Folktales in print are merely written representations of only part of the linguistic aspects of storytelling events. Folk cultural communication occurs only when it takes place in natural context. Even some literary scholars recognize that "the value of the study of the folklore . . . depends entirely on the context and the critical implications of the subject."[4]

Similarly, then, a folk craft cannot be communicated in totality in print, or even on videotape. This study, consequently, while attempting to describe and to discuss Homer Ledford's dulcimer craft, cannot hope to render to the reader the totality of the craft itself. Through such media as print or even videotape it is impossible for a viewer to see every angle of a process, to assess precisely the amount of pressure to place on an object in a phase of its delicate construction, to ascertain the "just right" angle of a pocketknife or chisel, to *feel* the wood or other materials—to know by personal immediate presence everything one must know to comprehend the craft and the craftsman and how they meet to produce art.

Thus far this delineation of the characteristics of popular, elite, and folk cultural modes has primarily emphasized the acquiring of cultural knowledge rather than the demonstration of that knowledge, although, of course, acquiring cultural learning and expressing cultural learning are in reality two sides of one coin. Because this study deals specifically with the production of a craft-art form and its artist-craftsman, it will perhaps be most pertinent to discuss the demonstration or expression of each of the three cultural systems in terms of art and craft products, and their artists-performers-makers.

In order to achieve success—that is, to make money—in the popular-culture system, artists-craftsmen-performers and their products (especially the latter) must be faddish, innovative, and able to provide their mass audiences with immediately appealing, easily digestible entertainment or diversion; the audiences of the mass media are, for the most part, passive receivers of popular art forms and will expend little intellectual effort in order to appreciate them. The norms for popular-culture art forms are determined by popular demand, by what will work or succeed with the mass public, by what will be accepted as the "in" thing; few, if any, codified rules govern such art forms. Consequently, popular art is continually changing and necessarily ephemeral; the minute an art product of popular culture ceases to attract the masses, popular culture permits and even demands that such a form be changed, altered, or obliterated; incessant—sometimes frenzied—mass popularity is the ideal goal. Obviously, such adulation can persist for only a relatively brief span of time; hence the continual flux and ephemeral nature of popular culture products. Furthermore, in its efforts to remain continually in vogue, popular culture frequently borrows forms, styles, and modes from both elite and folk culture and then subjects the borrowing to some sort of faddish alteration; hence such hybrids as "folk rock." This preoccupation with fad and fashion is in sharp contrast to folk and elite art forms, both of which endure over long periods of time.

In the elite-culture system, technical and thematic complexities are a great concern in art forms; as a result, audiences are usually instructed formally in proper "appreciation," often through so-called music or art or literature appreciation courses. Audiences are expected to ponder and savor each production, to experience it over and over again. Ideally, once an elite art form is created, it does not change; performances generally are attempts to reproduce as exactly as possible the original creation as conceived by its author; one would not, for example, attempt to rework a Beethoven symphony. Rules for both the creation and the performance of elite art forms are often strictly codified; however, within such codified techniques, individualistic variation is usually permitted, allowing authors and artists to develop idiosyncratic approaches to style and content. Consequently, it is possible, for instance, to recognize the works of various given individuals, all of whom might nonetheless by painting within one mode; for example, one can differentiate among the many Florentine masters and identify any one master's works, yet all such artists are still within the Florentine "school." Furthermore, all of these elite art forms, once created, persist through time and space. Maintained and perpetuated by elite institutions—such as libraries, universities and other schools, museums, collectors, and patrons of the arts— they endure for long periods of time.

In contrast, the art forms of folk culture historically have not been maintained and preserved by museums and other institutions as have been elite art forms. Still, folk culture persists, and its art forms are also enduring; indeed, in some cases, folk art forms endure for longer periods of time than do elite art forms; consider, for example, the counting-out rhyme "eeny meeny miny mo," dating from the time of the Druids.[5] A given folk art form persists and is perpetuated not in institutions—although more and more museums are now collecting folk-culture items—but rather in the viable, perpetual, but ever-changing sociocultural milieu in which it originated. That is, each person who knows or shares folk culture perpetuates it; in a manner of speaking, then, people themselves constitute the repositories— the "libraries," "museums," "collections," and so on—for folk-culture art forms, and indeed all folk knowledge. To continue with the same metaphor, each time someone performs, creates, shares, or otherwise communicates folk culture, it amounts to a display or showcase of that material—just as elite culture is displayed, performed, or communicated in opera houses, museums, galleries, classrooms, and the like, and popular culture is communicated by the commercial mass media.

Yet there exists a profound difference between the nature of folk cultural communication and that of either elite or popular culture. Each time a folk-culture art form is shared, it is—to use Phillips Barry's term—*recreated*.[6] Unlike elite art, folk art changes each time it is performed, demonstrated, or constructed. Yet folk art does not change completely, does not change to the point that the particular form is unrecognizable; in the Hispanic Southwest, for instance, there are seemingly limitless varieties of religious carvings—all of which are, in spite of their diversity, called *Santos*.[7] Likewise, there are many sizes, shapes, colors—indeed conceptions—of what we call dulcimers, yet they are all still dulcimers.[8] Each time Homer constructs a dulcimer, he performs his task differently from other dulcimer makers; even when he recreates the same traditional style over and over again, each process of construction and its product will be different. Yet all are traditional dulcimers; indeed, each, though different, is nonetheless *his* traditional dulcimer. It is this re-creative change *within* a traditional format that to a great extent sets folk art forms apart from elite art forms that do not change and popular art forms that constantly change completely, usually to the point of obscurity; that is, forms in popular culture are ephemeral.[9] Indeed, the re-creation or change inherent in a folk culture's art forms might be called its *sine qua non*; it is the re-creative change that keeps a given folk-culture form viable, constantly adaptable to the inevitable flux in its sociocultural milieu.

Unlike elite art, the creation or performance of folk art forms is governed not by codified rules, but rather by tacitly or spontaneously accepted traditions, which are nevertheless often followed as strictly as are elite culture's most explicit codes. Many of the progenitors and re-creators or perpetuators of folk culture are unknown, or anonymous to larger society, unlike the celebrities of elite or popular cutlure. Folk performers-artists-craftsmen however, often have a personal, even intimate, relationship with their audiences—unlike either elite or popular artists—and are free to re-create the art piece and thereby to alter it to some extent.

Given this delineation of the characteristics of the three systems of culture in our society, two points should be stressed. First, it must be understood that one cannot make value judgments cross-culturally. Different cultures, no matter how similar they may appear, are not the same and should not be judged or evaluated as though they were. Indeed, no such universal, platonic set of criteria exists. The most that can be said is that various cultures are different—not better or worse, but just *different*. One can then proceed to delineate the differences. Admittedly, such a culturally pluralistic and relativistic stance is difficult to maintain, as witnessed, for example, in the analytic category of "primitive," a term now happily falling into disuse. Consequently, many shortsighted observers of American elite, popular, and folk cultures fall prey to the ethnocentric trap and tend to rank them hierarchically, with folk usually relegated to the bottom, popular not far above, and elite at the apex.[10] (Indeed, even the word *elite* implies such ranking; it should probably be changed to "institutionalized" or some other appropriate term.)

The second point to be stressed, or restressed, is that the cultural systems are not mutually exclusive. Of the three, popular culture probably borrows most from the other two and folk culture the least, but all three overlap, and each borrows to some extent from the other two; for example, a folkcraft like Homer's may be infused with elements of both elite and popular culture.[11] In our complex society, no cultural system or its products are unaffectd by the other two cultural systems and their products.[12]

Consequently, in order to analyze and classify any one phenomenon as primarily a product of folk, popular, or elite culture, it is essential to consider the components of that phenomenon that work together in a more or less unified and structured way to create it. Eight such interdependent components—performer, audience, intent, function, text, texture, context,and origin,[13]—will be used in discussing Homer's craft, employing the following understanding of the meaning of the terms.

The *performer*, of course, is the person (or persons) who creates or exhibits the phenomenon, event, or artifact—the who of the situation. The *audience* is the person or group for whom or to whom a thing is done. *Intent* is the reason why a thing is done or why it exists. Closely related to intent is *function*, which is what actually happens when the phenomenon takes place or exists, the effects of the cultural item being analyzed. *Text* is the thing itself—the artifact, folksong, belief, or what have you. *Texture* is the how, the manner in which the artifact is created or the performance or exhibition accomplished. *Context* is the where, the entire sociocultural milieu and physical environment in which the text is performed or created or located. *Origin* is, of course, the traceable beginnings of any phenomenon of culture.

As stated earlier, these eight components are interdependent; when one changes, it is quite likely that others will also change, and the result may be a complete alteration of the nature of the phenomenon; culture, as a process of learning and expressing, as a process of communication, is subject to the laws of structured phenomena.[14] For example, a radical modification of the folkcraft of dulcimer making can be found in various woodcraft catalogs advertising dulcimer kits, with which folk musical instruments can allegedly be built. One such catalog states, "Your family and friends will love the Kentucky Bluegrass sound of this easy to play Appalachian Heart-Shaped Dulcimer!"[15] Such a statement reveals a lack of knowledge and appreciation of the traditional folk dulcimer; its sound is very different from that of typical bluegrass instruments. Moreover, the instrument itself, as advertised, is obviously not of folk provenience. Consisting of mass-produced parts—including metal tuning pegs—and sold through mass-marketing techniques, this kit can in no way be used to produce a folk-culture instrument. The intent, function, text, texture, and context of these dulcimer kits have been so divorced from folk cultural modes that the resulting instrument can no longer be considered a traditional Appalachian dulcimer.

This is not to say that in modern society a folkcraft, or its craftsman, must be completely free of all influences from or reflections of popular or elite culture in order to remain a product of the folk cultural process; such "purity" cannot exist in our complex industrialized world. However, the tools of analysis and classification outlined above make it possible to identify folk, popular, and elite influences upon a craft and then to classify that product as primarily folk, popular, or elite. As with all products of folk culture, however, the Appalachian dulcimer—the text—has necessarily been affected by contact with elite and popular cultural systems. An excellent example of popular influence upon the dulcimer craft is the recent tendency on the part of some craftsmen to use guitar-type frets on dulcimers. That such frets are not traditional can be verified by examining various old dulcimers in museums; these have small wire frets, many made out of little brass safety pins, hammered down into the fingerboard.[16] Unfortunately, many newer dulcimer makers and their customers are more familiar with the guitars, mandolins, and banjos produced by popular culture than with the traditional characteristics of the Appalachian dulcimer.[17]

A similar example of popular-culture influences upon the traditional dulcimer craft is the practice of placing mechanical steel pegs or guitar-type tuning keys on a dulcimer rather than the traditional wooden pegs set in a hollowed-out pegbox. The attempt to electrify a dulcimer is yet another example of popular and elite cultures' influence upon the folk instrument.[18]

At times, influences from popular or elite culture can so alter a folkcraft that the resulting product, or "text," can no longer be considered a folkcraft. For example, Sears, Roebuck and some foreign manufacturers have begun mass-producing "Appalachian dulcimers" and selling them via mail-order catalogs. Such production and marketing practices represent popular culture's exploitation of the popularity of a folk-culture instrument, accomplished by the use of elite cultural knowledge to produce the instruments on a mass basis so that they can be commercially marketed on a mass scale. The intent is the *raison d'être* of all popular culture—that is, to make money—but the result is that these instruments are no longer a part of the folk cultural process; they are what Richard Dorson has called "fakelore" (obviously imitation folkloric phenomena) or what Tom Sullenberger terms "folklure" (fakelore blatantly used for popular commercial gain).[19]

Because a craft does not exist in the abstract, it cannot be realistically separated from the craftsman who practices it, and that individual, too, is exposed to the influence of popular and elite cultural systems. A superb example of accommodation by folk craftsmen to popular and elite culture is documented by Michael Owen Jones in his study of Appalachian chairmakers.[20] After the introduction of linoleum—a product of both elite chemical and industrial knowledge and popular mass-marketing techniques—some folk craftsmen changed the way they constructed the feet of chairs, because the older style of feet cut into the linoleum. The redesigned chairs, however, did not necessarily cease to be folkcraft, nor did their creators necessarily cease to be folk craftsmen merely because the chairs had been altered somewhat to accommodate a product of elite and popular cultures.[21] In all such instances, one must critically scrutinize first the craftsman (the performer, including his intent) and his craft (the text, including its function) and then the context in which the craft is created, how it is created (texture) and for whom it is created (audience) in order to determine whether a particular craft, originally designated as a folk process, remains predominantly such in spite of influences from other cultural systems.

To begin such an analysis of Homer Ledford and his Appalachian

craft, one must first determine why and how Homer became a dulcimer craftsman. Homer was born and raised in a rural mountainous
area of Tennessee; there can be no doubt that his home background,
and by extension his early orientation to life, was predominantly
created by folk cultural systems. This is not to say that influences
from other cultural systems were nonexistent; Homer did go to public
schools—elite-culture institutions—where he learned, among other
things, songs considered by his teachers to be "folk" music. Probably
a more enduring impression and influence than the schools upon
Homer, however, as far as music was concerned, was provided by wax
recordings and a battery-powered radio—both popular-culture media.
Via these media Homer became familiar with the music played by
performers from the Grand Ole Opry and by what he now calls "old-
style" performances such as those by Buell Kazee. As noted in Part
I, scholars have recognized that such "old-style" music, even though
transmitted by popular culture's media, nonetheless constituted a
legitimate folkloric influence for its listeners during the years of the
so-called hillbilly music "watershed,"[22] when Homer was growing
up. In terms of our analytic components, the broadcasting or studio
context of such performances was definitely not folk, but a mixture
of elite and popular culture. Yet the performers could very often be
classified as folk artists, and much of the music was at least derived
from folk culture. The audience, either in a studio or at the Grand
Ole Opry, was certainly not folk but a mixture of popular and elite
cultures. Yet it seems that the audience listening to such music in
their homes might still be considered folk, even though there were
media apparatus and miles of space between them and the performer.
In any event, the function of the music learned via such media
definitely was folkloric, as it was adopted and adapted and perpetuated
in folkloric music-making situations by listeners in their own homes
or local gathering places. In many instances, even the intent of such
early media performances was not solely the popular-culture drive
to make money. As Homer says, "Many of the performers simply
wanted to play the music they grew up with for others who also appreciated it, and if some 'sponsor' wanted to pay them for it, then
so much the better." Their performances were often of unmistakable
folk texture, although as years passed, many performers became more
and more influenced by both popular and elite styles. So it seems that
a good portion of Homer's exposure to music on early radio and recordings can still be seen as folkloric in nature.

However, Homer was also exposed to music nearly exclusively
through folk cultural modes—play-parties, itinerant musicians, local

performers, and the one-week shape note "school" taught by his uncle. Indeed, Homer's overall playing development was based upon these personal relationships, as they preceded the purchase of either the phonograph player or radio. However, eventually Homer utilized all cultural resources—folk, popular, and elite—to further develop his unusual musical talent.

In addition to his love for music, Homer displayed even as a young boy a penchant for working with wood. Through trial and error, imitation of other folk craftsmen around him, and innumerable hours of patient practice, he had become a folk craftsman of reputation even before he left his mountain community.

When Homer attended the John C. Campbell Folk School—which must be considered an elite institution—he saw, for the first time, a traditional Appalachian dulcimer, and was taught to play it via a folk cultural process. Homer studied the construction of the dulcimer, and then, because he was already an accomplished craftsman and had already constructed several musical instruments, he applied his folk cultural knowledge to the construction of the dulcimer and simply copied or replicated what was before him; and, of course, replication—or imitation—is an authentic way of passing on tradition.

It is interesting to note the difference between popular and folk cultural processes as regards copying or imitation, or what George Kubler prefers (and I agree) to call replication: "The term 'replication' is a respectable old-fashioned word long in disuse, and we revive it here not only to avoid the negative judgment that adhers to the idea of 'copying' but also to include by definition that essential trait of repeating events which is trivial variation."[23] What Homer did with the traditional Appalachian dulcimer introduced to him at the school was to replicate its traditional form, with the slight variations that necessarily accompany any two separate phenomena plus a change in surface treatment resulting from his preference for a differnt sort of finish on a musical instrument. Homer's intention was to perpetuate the traditional object, to replicate it as a musical instrument traditional to his native culture, and in the process to expand further his own knowledge and abilities in the direction in which they were already developing—that of handcrafting musical instruments. As noted by most folklorists, folk cultural processes of learning, sharing, and perpetuating traditional knowledge include "informal demonstration or imitation" or even learning by "customary example."[24]

Such intentional *replication* differs markedly from the widespread, indiscriminate, mercenary, and profligate *copying* that accompanies popular culture's merchandising. While folk culture engages in conservative replication of quality traditional forms, with built-in planned permanence and evidence of personal attention by the craftsman, popular culture involves itself more with large-scale impersonal copying of objects, with built-in obsolescence. Kubler further notes the often inevitable degeneration of the copied object in mass-production-oriented popular culture: "Diminished quality becomes apparent when the maker reduces the excellence of the replica, either because of economic pressures or because of his inability to comprehend the full scope or import of the model [as in the case of factory-produced "dulcimers"]. . . . When a mass-produced article of good design begins to have a wider market and more intense competition, the manufacturers simplify its design to get the price down until the product is reduced to the fewest possible parts in a construction no more durable than necessary."[25] Homer, of course, was never in such a position; rather, existing as he was, primarily through folk cultural processes, Homer the young craftsman could readily assimilate the dulcimer craft, and do so without any direct guidance or popular culture involvement or motivation. Such folk cultural assimilation or replication was not copying in the popular culture sense; there was no mercenary motivation, no mechanical production line, no profligate or indiscriminate copying with plans to merchandise the object to the masses. The situation would have been no different had Homer found a long-stored dulcimer in some neighbor's attic.

If the craftsman who receives folk knowledge is already a folk craftsman, then there is no discontinuity in the folk cultural process. Whether a craftsman who has *not* learned his skill in the folk cultural process can also learn a folk-culture craft and produce it as a truly folk form is a moot question, each case having to be analyzed separately. Can, for instance, a skilled woodworker who has learned his trade solely in elite-culture contexts—schools, books, and so on—produce a dulcimer that can truly be considered a traditional Appalachian folk instrument? Can the undoubtedly skilled factory workers in Korea and Czechoslovakia produce "Appalachian dulcimers?" I do not believe the forms they produce can be called traditional Appalachian dulcimers; at best, they might be called "copies," "imitations," or "representations" of the traditional Appalachian dulcimer. *Learning by imitation* (or replication), as Homer did, and *producing an imitation*, as foreign manufacturers do, are quite different things.

Similarly, several craftsmen in this country—for example, natives of New York, Los Angeles, or Chicago—produce dulcimers they call traditional and Appalachian, yet many of these makers have learned

55. Summer, 1983

both their general skills and specific knowledge of dulcimers in shop classes, or even from books, outside of Appalachia. Can their instruments be called "traditional Appalachian dulcimers?" Again, I believe such objects to be essentially products of popular-culture processes, representative of popular culture's continual usurpation of folk culture forms. Henry Glassie observes: "The most usual result of the influence of popular culture upon folk material duing the past 130 years in America, and particularly the past fifty, has been the replacement of the traditional object by its popular equivalent." He further notes that "popular material objects may be based directly on folk models."[26] Certainly that is what has happened to the dulcimer; nearly every component of its "popular equivalent," it seems to me, is at odds with folk cultural characteristics. The "performer" is not folk; the audience is usually not folk; function and intent tend to be commercial or faddish; texture and context are usually not folk; only the text, the item itself, resembles a true folk form—but so do photographs of folk forms, yet they are not the forms themselves.

Another question presents itself: can a folk craftsman who has acquired his skills in a tradition quite different from the folk cultural process he is trying to learn produce a truly folk form? For example, could a maker of the Indian sitar, or the African flute or drum, make a traditional Appalachian dulcimer? In each case the maker could no doubt produce an instrument, but what would it *be*? What would be its significance? I believe that such an instrument would lack the significance of a truly traditional Appalachian dulcimer such as Homer's. For Homer's dulcimer craft is inextricably grounded in the sociocultural, psychological, socioeconomic, and political milieu of his youth; the almost destitute boy sitting and whittling and dreaming on the red cedar woodpile is indeed the father of the man who now practices a craft which sprang up and flourished in the southern Appalachians even as he himself did. Homer's entire life—from boyhood through manhood—has been inseparably bound up with his music and his instruments; hence his remark to the girl who almost stepped on one of his instruments that she would be "a-walking on" him.

How, then, could any craftsman of urban or foreign heritage produce the same dulcimer as Homer does? Even an exact physical copy of Homer's instrument would not be the same; it *could* not be the same; neither it nor its maker was ever nourished by the indigenous culture in the hills of Appalachia; neither mountain crafts nor mountain music could possibly have the same significance for such craftsmen as they do for Homer. Each dulcimer that Homer makes is an affirmation that he can have what others had in the towns he visited as a child. Downtrodden for years, Appalachian folk culture is, along with other minority cultures in this country, asserting itself; and for Homer his dulcimer is a source of pride in his own abilities and in his Appalachian folk heritage.

In a word, then, the significance of Homer's first work with the dulcimer was congruent with the original dulcimer craft. He, a traditional Appalachian craftsman and musician, made traditional Appalachian dulcimers for people who needed and wanted them to play for their own and others' pleasure. It makes little difference that the John C. Campbell Folk School was an elite institution; the two instruments to which Homer was first exposed—one he repaired and the other he played—were both traditional folk instruments, and his musical introduction to the instrument was through the traditional folk cultural process. Homer's experience at the school had little to do with attempts by elite- or popular-culture enthusiasts to "revive" folk culture (usually for profit) or to "revitalize" flagging or even defunct folk-culture processes.[27] Rather, Homer was a young folk craftsman and musician who merely expanded both his craft and his musical repertoire through folk cultural processes, though such expansion was indeed made possible by the gathering place provided by the John C. Campbell Folk School. In essence it was Mrs. Campbell's humanity—and her respect for Homer and his culture—and Edna Ritchie's enthusiasm and adeptness with the dulcimer that encouraged Homer to expand his craftsmanship and musical abilities to include the sweet-playing instrument; the elite institution merely provided the meeting place for Homer, Mrs. Campbell, Edna, and the Thomas dulcimers.

Later, of course, Homer attended college, again an elite institution. He did not go in order to learn the dulcimer craft, however, but to learn how to use modern electric woodworking tools and to learn the theories of pattern making and designing and so forth, thus adding another dimension to his already well-developed talents. Such influence from elite culture, however, does not mean that Homer's dulcimers ceased to be traditional; his instruments are to this day traditional Appalachian dulcimers constructed in a predominantly folk cultural mode.

The overall design—the text—of the Ledford dulcimer perhaps most resembles the instruments of J.E. Thomas. Jean Ritchie calls Homer "probably the best-known living member of the Thomas Family of dulcimer makers."[28] J. Edward Thomas is the earliest dulcimer maker and player scholars have been able to document to any extent in this country. He was born in 1850 in Letcher County, Kentucky, and lived most of his life in the little village of Bath; he began making dulcimers in 1871 and continued until shortly before his death in 1933, and his dulcimers are unquestionably among the finest examples of the traditional craft.[29]

Homer's techniques are strikingly similar to the Thomas construction,[30] and except for the modifications described in Part I, the basic design and construction of his dulcimers have remained essentially unchanged for over 30 years; as Homer explains, "I tried to hang onto the traditional ways." On a few occasions, Homer has acquiesced to a customer's insistence upon guitar-type frets or pegs, but in general, popular culture's influences have been minimal on Homer's craft. Elite culture's influences have been considerably greater.

When Homer first started making dulcimers he used "found" wood, just as he had for all of his craft products, and for several years he continued to construct instruments with whatever wood he had at his disposal. Gradually, as he started to have a little money to invest in his craft, Homer began to buy wood from lumbermills and woodworking supply houses—both partly elite- and partly popular-culture sources. Homer still prefers to use "found" wood whenever possible, but he has become more sophisticated in the process; for instance, he continually scouts for antique woods in structures that are being renovated or demolished, and then bargains with the owners for choice pieces. Also, whenever possible, he loves to "mark" certain trees, hoping to get the wood from them when they are mature enough to harvest; he has, I believe, future plans for some young wild cherry and black walnut trees in my back yard. So, even though he procures some of his wood from popular-culture outlets, he still uses and prefers folk processes.

One of the best examples of the influences of the different culture systems upon Homer's craft can be found in his dulcimer pegs. He buys Brazilian rosewood in the popular-culture mass market; he cuts out the basic shape of the peg with the machine tools of elite culture; but the top of the peg itself he hand carves with a pocketknife, which is certainly a folk cultural mode. Homer's standardization process in forming his pegs is an elite industrial technique, but the peg former with which he has standardized the stem of his pegs and the fret maker that cuts and forms his staple-type frets are inventions created by Homer within the folk cultural process, remarkable examples of the same folk genius that created the dulcimer itself and other folk cultural artifacts.

The fret maker is, as far as I can ascertain, an idea unique to

Homer; however, the idea of the peg former was certainly influenced by Homer's knowledge of the pencil sharpener, a concept that would probably be classified within the elite cultural mode. Homer's adaptation of elite cultural knowledge for a folk cultural purpose is a perfect example of *bricolage*—a process continually utilized in folk culture—whereby a new idea is analyzed and compared with old ones, and a composite idea is developed; that is, ideas or things are broken down into their respective components and then re-formed into something else for a new purpose.[31] Homer is fond of quoting from one of his former industrial arts teachers: "There's nothing new under the sun; you just rearrange it." Apparently agreeing with Homer and his professor, a prominent art historian says: "It is a truism that no work of art is completely original; that every artist, even the greatest, stands on the shoulders of the past. There is no artistic creation out of nothing; *ex nihilo nihil fit.*"[32] "A 'new' work of art, then, is largely formed of images and meanings which are already part of the collective understanding."[33] Homer utilizes this same process in the creation of his dulcimer clamps; he starts by cutting up a broomstick, which is usually sold and used as a popular culture item. From a commercial, mass-produced implement, Homer creates—via a folk process—something entirely different: a device to elaborate and refine his folk craft.

Because of Homer's use of his peg former, fret maker, and (especially) power tools, some purists contend that his craft is no longer traditional; such pedantic scholarship often views folk culture as static or as a "thing" rather than as a process of learning and possessing knowledge and expressing that knowledge.[34] Other scholars who have studied Appalachian craftsmen adamantly maintain that such practices in a traditional folk culture craft alter the status neither of the folkcraft nor of the traditional craftsmen. For example, Michael Owen Jones asserts that "the products of 'folk' industry are not automatically rendered 'non-folk' . . . simply because of a change in tools, materials, or techniques of construction, or owing to a change in the expressive qualities of the products." Rather, "industrialization has brought about some alterations in the tools and techniques of craft work which have reduced some of the physical labor involved in production, introduced a degree of standardization in the products, enlarged the variety of things produced, and satisfied more fully the growing demands for the products." In addition, urbanization "has created a consumer public with different values needing fulfillment which has resulted in the creation of a greater variety of objects, the encouragement of innovation, and the generation of new objects, designs, and stylistic traits, and it has stimulated the production of objects that might otherwise, owing to industrialization, have disappeared."[35] Generally concurring with Jones, Charles Joyner, in his survey of North Carolina dulcimer makers, observes:

> They are traditional craftsmen, despite the influence of various forms of popular culture. None of them are strangers to power tools, television, or Sears and Roebuck catalogues. Most of them are acquainted, through craft fairs, with a variety of other craftsmen. Most of them know each other's work. Folk culture is not defined by its lack of contact with popular culture . . . folk culture is partially defined by its cultural conservatism, its tendency to preserve the past within the present, rather than to change. But folk culture is not static. Indeed it is partially defined by change, by variation, as well as by conservatism. Most folklorists take the lack of variation in a given item as a sure sign that the item has not been governed in its development by traditional processes, in other words that it is not folk.[36]

Such views are corroborated by a prominent art historian who supports not only the freedom of the artist to employ different procedures and to experiment with new materials, but also to earn money from his activity: "There is no good reason to specify that art must be made or executed by hand and not by machinery . . . that art must be made or performed by some particular technique, of some particular material, by the free imagination, with no thought of gain."[37] Too often the criterion "free from commercial activity" has been used as a component in defining folk culture. Yet nearly all folk cultural processes involve economic consideration: trading, bartering, and selling have been an intricate part of folk cultural processes from time immemorial. It is true that the commercial aspects of folk culture are quite different from those of popular culture. In popular culture the profit impetus is paramount; in folk culture satisfaction of needs, whether utilitarian or artistic or some combination of both, is the principal underlying motivation, and moneymaking—while welcome and necessary and often definitely planned—is not the central focus. Yet folk culture necessarily operates in association with the other two systems; commercial interaction is merely one of the ways the cultural systems mesh, and folk processes involve intercultural as well as intracultural economic activities.[38]

The adoption of selected aspects of one cultural system by another

56. View of Homer's shop

does not necessarily change the adopting system's nature, especially as the adopting system usually adapts the adopted aspects to its own needs. For example, Homer adopts machinery and tools, mainly from elite culture, but then adapts them—usually altering them substantially—to his dulcimer craft; indeed, often his modifications are so extensive that one could nearly say that the tools then become part of Homer's traditional craft. Homer's own answer to the notion that power tools invalidate the traditionality of his craft is simple: he maintains that traditional mountain craftsmen of years past would have used power equipment had it been available to them; the only reason they did not use it was that it was not at their disposal. When asked about making money from his craft, Homer seemed puzzled: "Nearly all the old mountain craftsmen traded or sold what they made. I can't see that there's anything wrong with that. A person has to eat!"

Homer does realize that his elite-culture training could, if wrongly used, create a dulcimer no longer within the folk cultural mode. Consequently, Homer consciously tempers his use of elite knowledge and tools so that he he will not alter the traditional "text" of the Appalachian mountain dulcimer. For example, the context in which Homer constructs his dulcimers is as traditional as one could wish it to be in this day and age. His shop (figs. 56 and 57) is in the basement of his home; it is, and will remain, a one-man operation like those of most mountain craftsmen; and Homer lavishes hand work on each dulcimer. Although the texture of Homer's dulcimer craft has in some ways been influenced by elite and popular cultures, the craft itself has remained essentially traditional; that is, Homer's knowledge of how to make the dulcimer, what it should look like, how it should sound and play—the *essentials* of his dulcimer craft—have remained basically the same. Even more important, the way Homer feels about his craft has never changed.

Homer's love of music and woodworking, and his identification with his craft and his instruments, have been documented time and again throughout this study. His long-term intimacy with the dulcimer craft is perhaps a fundamental distinguishing characteristic of the folk cultural mode, in revealing contrast to the popular culture expectations of the young man from the Northeast who wanted to learn the dulcimer craft in one week so he could construct the instruments for a living. Such a goal was impossible, of course, just as it would be impossible for a stranger to learn, in one week, a regional argot with its dialect and nuances of meaning—a perfect example of folk culture—and then to speak as would a native of the area. Folk culture is not learned in one week, nor is it learned by "strangers;" rather it is absorbed over years and years of intimate relationship. This kind of informal intimacy is usually not present in popular-culture systems—neither in their learning processes nor in their expressions of that learning; and in elite culture, intimacy is scheduled, codified, regimented, prescribed as part of elite learning and expression; but Homer's dulcimer craft is intimately integrated into the entire fabric of his life, and such an intimacy is accomplished only within the folk cultural traditional processes:

> My whole life has been music and making things . . . it seems like I eat and breathe and sleep and everything my work and sometimes too much . . . all day and some of the night. I'm not always *making* something; sometimes a lot of folks do come and want to see something or whatever, or play . . . I don't know, all total it takes up maybe 75 percent, or maybe more, which is pretty high; doesn't leave much for the family, does it? . . . but you touch a lot of people's lives when they come to you—though you might not plan on doing it, you do.

Emanating from Homer's feelings about his craft and about his instruments is his demonstrated intent to preserve and to extol the traditionality of the mountain dulcimer. Homer does not want to popularize his dulcimer, does not strive to make it "folksy," does not adopt the souvenir shop approach to either craftsmanship or marketing. Every modification that Homer has made in his dulcimer has been accomplished with his intention to make the instrument even better musically, functionally, or aesthetically while preserving the traditional nature of the instrument. Homer will normally acquiesce to a customer's wishes for nontraditional features but does not usually like the finished product; each time that I have heard him comment about such a custom product, he has referred to it as "so-and-so's dulcimer" rather than his own; he tends not to want to identify himself with it.

The manner in which Homer has adapted yet kept intact the traditional form of the dulcimer exemplifies what Kubler calls "replication of the prime" in such a fashion as to permit serial individuality without destroying the original form: "It is in the nature of being that no event ever repeats, but it is in the nature of thought that we understand events only by the identities we imagine among them," so that with traditional phenomena we see displayed "the idea of a linked succession of prime works with replications, all being distributed in

57. View of Homer's shop

time as recognizably early and late versions of the same kind."[39]
M.O. Jones's remarks in his study of traditional folk chairmakers aptly
serve to summarize Kubler's views as they pertain to Homer's freedom
to innovate *within* the traditional dulcimer craft and within the con-
fines of the dulcimer form:

> What tends to happen in utilitarian art is that the producer
> accepts a traditional framework and form so that he can direct
> his thoughts and creative energy to the surface decoration or
> refinement of that form. . . . the majority of artists accept
> basic conceptions and techniques and fundamentals of style,
> and they produce a few variations within this general
> framework. In addition, the values of the audience or con-
> sumer public often emphasize stability of form, especially in
> utilitarian forms which, according to precedence, are satisfac-
> tory for their useful purposes in the present form.[40]

Therefore, Homer is somewhat compelled by his audience, as well
as by his reverence for traditional form, to perpetuate that which is
considered not only traditional but functional. When his innovative
and creative drives alter the dulcimer to the point that it is scarcely
recognizable as such, the resulting newly created object must be
named something else—such as his dulcitar and his dulcibro.[41]

The basic Ledford dulcimer is looked upon as a traditional Appalachian musical instrument, and one of the best examples of its
kind. It has served to bring pride to the small town in which Homer
resides; it has created a sense of pride and awe in its owners. It has
been purchased by people from nearly every walk of life throughout
the world; professional performers, school bands and music depart-
ments, and even the Smithsonian have acquired Homer's instruments.
The Ledford dulcimer is displayed in craft shops in the Appalachian
region; it has prompted invitations for Homer to appear at fairs, lead
workshops, and even teach classes in dulcimer construction; he has
been interviewed and photographed by newspapers, journals, and the
National Geographic, and videotaped for educational television. In
a word, society has recognized and celebrated Homer's dulcimer, il-
lustrating Jones's contention that "industrialism has been attended
by a growing dissatisfaction, among many people, with mass-produced
objects and by a desire for handmade things, thus stimulating hand
production rather than destroying it. The hypothesis that making or
doing things in daily life was brought to an end by industrialization
or urbanization has little to recommend it."[42]

In his study of North Carolina dulcimer makers, Charles Joyner comments that those traditional mountain craftsmen "are all conscious of carrying on a great tradition. They share with the folklorist a sense of precious traditions on the verge of extinction; but do not share his sense of irony that the revival of dulcimer making in Appalachia is a direct outgrowth of popular culture's interest in the instrument, nor his concern that popular culture is extremely fickle."[43]

However, Homer does not believe, nor do I, that popular culture is responsible for the continued interest in the dulcimer. It is true that many dulcimer customers are primarily popular-culture adherents or proponents; not everyone who buys a dulcimer lives his life predominantly by what we call folk culture; indeed, very few people could today be so classified. As complex human beings living in a complex society, everything that we are, and all that we do— motivations, aspirations, guidelines, knowledge and expression, behavior—is a *mixture* of what analysts call folk, popular, and elite cultures. Thus all peoples have some propensity for folk-culture products. As Jones notes, neither popular- nor elite-culture products satisfy the desires that some people experience for more personalized, humanized possessions. This helps to explain the widespread acceptance of the dulcimer in today's complex society.

Irving Sloane observes: "Currently, the dulcimer is enjoying a lively renaissance with much popular interest in its history, music, and construction. Much of this has to do with its simple charm and ease of playing, but the dulcimer more than any other instrument wears an aura of nostalgia, a wistful echo of some legendary time when graciousness, sentiment, and repose gave a more secure sense of one's place in the scheme of things."[44] Such sentiments, of course, belong more to the conservative world of folk culture than to the hurly-burly of popular culture; unfortunately the longing for folk cultural modes is too often expressed and satisfied in nostalgia, but this should not be interpreted to mean that folk culture is itself nostalgic. Rather, modern man, being oriented predominantly to popular-culture products, modes, and processes, tends to misinterpret folk culture's products, modes, or processes as nostalgic. Such association is in the mind and feelings of the interpreter, not in folk culture itself, which is constantly changing, adapting to its contemporary social milieux. The satisfaction to be found in folk culture lies in its ability to involve the individual, or at least to permit appreciation of the involvement, more intimately in a meaningful experience than can popular culture.

The satisfaction that comes from owning and using a handcrafted object is enhanced when something of the personal history of the maker is known; indeed, the object becomes even more significant for its owners or users when its folk cultural history is appreciated. This is simply not the case with mass-produced or copied objects, even ones that might perhaps appear to be physically "identical" to a folk-culture product. To test this hypothesis, simply hand someone a Ledford dulcimer and tell him or her a little about it and its maker; then do the same with a catalog-ordered, factory-produced dulcimer copy and compare reactions. Such appreciation is not the expression of a popular cultural mode of communicative behavior but folk cultural; the modern revival of dulcimer making is not a direct outgrowth of popular culture's interest in the instrument but the result of a reawakening or rediscovering of folk cultural propensities. A similar display is manifest in the do-it-yourself projects of "midnight" or "Saturday" mechanics; the folk cultural aspects of our individual personalities, according to Loyal Jones, prompt us to "want to do things for ourselves, whether or not it is practical. . . . There is satisfaction in that, in this age when people hire other people to do most of their work and supply their entertainment."[45]

The mixture of popular-culture and folk-culture desires and patterns of behavior is primarily responsible for Homer's being pressured recently to sell dulcimer "kits." Some customers insisted that though they very much desire a Ledford dulcimer they prefer to buy a disassembled one that they can put together and finish themselves. On the one hand, the notion that items for sale should be available in a standardized format is, of course, a central aspect of popular culture's merchandising practices; on the other hand, the proclivity for doing or making things oneself is a manifestation of folk-culture influences; the two attitudes converge in the popularity of kits.

Homer cannot understand how people would prefer a kit dulcimer to his own handcrafted instrument, as the price for the kit is not much less. Nor does he consider a kit dulcimer to have nearly the quality of his finished instrument; it can at best be called a "copy" of Homer's Appalachain dulcimer. Homer does not want to become known as a kit manufacturer. He considers the whole kit business something of a novelty for the mass audience, which demands continuous novelty and easy accessibility; the folk audience prefers the familiar and personally involving.

Modern owners of Homer's own handcrafted traditional dulcimer—his "audience"—are not dissimilar to their counterparts in Homer's youth:

Back in the days of more isolation—the mountains when I was growing up—there was a great need for a musical instrument, something to strum along, simple, that could be made by hand; and. . . . whoever was handiest with tools did it and came up with some kind of musical instrument. . . . We had music at all the gatherings. . . . There was your total social thing—folk games, music, play-parties, dancing—and there was always a musical instrument of some sort; if it wasn't a dulcimer it was a fiddle, or a homemade banjo.

People still buy dulcimers because they love a handmade object and because they love music, the original motivations that prompted Homer to make musical instruments. Society has changed, though, and cultural processes always reflect social flux. Homer no longer constructs instruments for only his own and his relatives', friends', and neighbors' use; the social network of which Homer now finds himself a part is not only more extensive, in terms of both distance and time, but also often more intensive—requiring more knowledge and detail for its satisfaction and perpetuation—and assuredly more complex, demanding an increasing number of contacts and relationships of all sorts.

There is seldom a day, or night, that people do not stop by Homer's home. Some come to buy instruments or accessories, to obtain advice about their instruments or to discuss musical arrangements, or simply to see what sort of man makes that beautiful little dulcimer. Others want to interview him or document his craft (of course, this study took up some of Homer's time). Homer has so many visitors that he is almost always behind schedule in filling his orders, yet he believes that all of these demands on his time constitute an important aspect of his craft. After all, he feels, he makes things for *people*—who may be strangers when they arrive but not when they leave. The truth is that Homer relishes human interaction, especially if it entails his music and his craft, in contrast to the popular-culture artist who, as described by C. Wright Mills, "tends to be culturally trapped by his own success. . . . a leader of fashions he is himself subject to fashion. Moreover, his success as a star depends upon his 'playing the market;' he is not in any educative interplay with publics that support his development. By virtue of his success, The Star too becomes a marketeer."[46]

In other words, Homer and other folk-culture artists, performers, and craftsmen are truly involved with their audiences, whereas the popular culture personality is almost completely dominated and

58. A portrait of Homer and Colista at home

manipulated by his audience. Yet to some extent even the folk artist is "trapped" by his traditions. As Munro notes, "From the social and historical standpoint, the main reason why humanity patronizes the arts and pays the artist is because it finds his products valuable in aesthetic or other ways, not in order to give him the pleasure of expressing himself."[47] Still, the folk artist does individualize his product within its accepted forms, he does express himself, and certainly the performer-audience relationship is more extensive and more intimate in folk than in popular culture.

Homer is not the first Appalachian craftsman to experience involvement with modern complex society; it seems fairly certain that even Ed Thomas made dulcimers for people all over the world. The hypothesis that Appalachia was an isolated, somehow retarded sociocultural complex is fast falling into disuse.[48] Also to be discarded are the stereotypical notions that each family in Appalachian settlement pockets made everything they owned for themselves and their neighbors, and that each home had a dulcimer or other homemade instrument which would be played nightly—probably by a tobacco-chewing or pipe-smoking old granny—in front of a crackling fire in the cool of the mountain air; such stereotypical romantic concoctions should be left to local color literary artists, who, for the most part, were the progenitors of them. Most Appalachian families bought, traded, bartered, or won most of their possessions—a goodly number of which were, it is true, handmade by someone else. That someone else was usually a craftsman, or seamstress, or farrier—a tradesperson who made things or performed services people wanted and needed in everyday life. As Michael Owen Jones notes, such tradespeople were relatively scarce: "Only a few individuals now or in the past have engaged in such behavior occupationally . . . because the vocation of making things by hand, which is also a mode of expressive behavior, requires commitment to and involvement in the creative act."[49] Those who excelled were rewarded by their "audiences"—their customers—in increased sales, brought about usually by word-of-mouth advertisement. This is precisely the manner in which Homer has expanded his dulcimer craft; he has never advertised other than through the small brochure that he provides with each dulcimer he sells; yet he usually has more orders than he can fill on schedule, and his customers have been located throughout the world, not just in Appalachia. When questioned about why he thinks people buy his dulcimers, Homer replied:

About ten years ago many people bought them because it seemed the thing to do . . . maybe to put on the wall to decorate with; or they could have it for a good conversation piece. . . . But it seems like most of my customers today really play them. It's a simple instrument to play, and they say, "I can really play that." They'll tell you that very nearly every time. . . . A lot of the young folks can already play, and they've got their money now and are ready to get their dulcimer. I don't know how many of them have saved up for two or three years. . . . And, boy, you talk about tickled; they're just as pleased when they get it. It really makes me feel good to see

them so happy; and I know my dulcimer is going to be put
to good use.

People buy dulcimers for the same reasons they have always bought
them, and they want quality. Happily, only a few people, usually urban romantics, believe that handmade Appalachian crafts should be
rough and crude. Decrying the misguided tendency among some to
yield to what he calls a "base is beautiful" evaluation of folk-culture
products, Michael Owen Jones notes that, sadly and strangely, some
who harbor such misconceptions are museologists and others who
should have a more culturally pluralistic and relativistic perspective.[50]

Even the Appalachian customers of years past were quite
sophisticated in their evaluation of quality; they preferred finely
crafted objects, and bought them. Loyal Jones notes that in the mountains "there was fine exceptional craftsmanship in items . . . such
as . . . dulcimers which were played with great skill."[51] What is different about Homer's audience is the relative degree of affluence and
the fact that modern communication and transportation permit people from distant locations to be potential customers; but the cultural
impetus to possess and play a beautiful handmade musical instrument seems to have been constant through the years, and the *essential nature* of Homer's relationships with his audience is that which
he maintained in the beginning. His operation has simply changed
as society has changed—a process of adaptation aptly commented
upon and documented by Michael Owen Jones:

> Art promotes the interest of a group by virtue of the expressive
> qualities in the objects; and the artist, whose livelihood
> depends on the sale of the products to others, tends to objec-
> tify those values and ideas in his works. Therefore, a "folk"
> artist, or an individual who tends to create within a system
> of traditional and conventionalized modes of expression, may
> be sensitive to cultural drift or urbanization in order to create
> objects congenial with the contemporary values of a particular
> group. [Nonetheless] the "folk" artist is not suddenly "non-
> folk" the moment he invents or innovates within tradition
> and convention; his products are not "non-folk" because they
> appeal to consumers outside his immediate community; and
> change resulting from external pressures does not necessar-
> ily destroy the art tradition although alterations may
> occur.[52]

As the nature of society changes, so too the nature of cultural processes in society; some such changes often involve innovation.

To discuss innovation, change, and tradition as facets of the same phenomenon may appear incongruous; yet the creative urge—innovation—is at some point the very matrix of even traditional patterns; and change, which has been well documented in various folkloric patterns, is part of the dynamic essence of the traditional form within which it occurs.[53] In one respect what we are calling "folk culture" could be equated with "tradition," popular culture with "change," and elite culture with "innovation." Yet each cultural system has aspects of the other two. Folk culture, while predominantly traditional, is also mildly innovative and undergoes slow change; popular culture, while predominantly changeable or ephemeral, is also somewhat innovative and tends on occasion to be mildly traditional; elite culture, while predominantly innovative—progress toward new knowledge being the key—is also quite traditional with its proven processes, but will change abruptly for improvements in technique, breakthroughs in knowledge, and so on.

The terms *change, innovation,* and *tradition* will be used in the ensuing discussion as follows: change refers to the alteration, modification, rearrangement, or even eradication of an inherited style, design, form, process, or material; innovation is the creative invention of new styles, designs, forms, processes, or materials; tradition refers to the conservative perpetuation and replication of folk cultural phenomena. Obviously, the two processes of change and innovation are more than compatible, indeed are often intricately intertwined and frequently congruent.

Folklorists and other analysts of sociocultural phenomena must realize that folk cultural traditions do not exist in a vacuum or a museum sequestered from exposure and interaction with other sociocultural processes. Change is the essence of all life; if a thing does not change, it becomes stagnant, and tradition is not stagnation; the more currently viable a traditional process is, the more it will be subject to change. Sociocultural change will, over time, alter traditional or folk cultural forms, and at any given time these forms will reflect new sociocultural reality. What is worthy of wonderment is that they change so little. Generally, their basic elements endure as the essential components, the skeleton, the *sine qua non*, of the phenomenon. However, a craftsman or performer involved with traditional phenomena is certainly not rigidly or immutably bound by that tradition; rather he or she is under the constant influences of sociocultural flux, the proclivities of the audience, and his or her own needs and preferences. When Homer consciously strives to maintain the traditional aspects of his craft, he is in some degree tempering these various motivations for change.[54]

Accepted as nearly a commonplace among folklorists is the tenet that traditional *forms* in folk culture remain relatively intact, even though they may exist in numerous versions; indeed one folklorist states that traditional form is "the least changing of an object's components."[55] The traditional Appalachian dulcimer is a remarkable example of the perpetuation of "essential" elements, with "nonessential" elements undergoing change through time and over space. Charles Joyner notes that "craftsmen have not only preserved traditional forms and patterns, they have also adapted traditional methods to new materials and new techniques to old materials to create new forms and patterns of their own."[56] Such change and innovation, however, do not mean that traditional forms are altered completely. For example, Homer says that "the hourglass shape is the way a dulcimer really ought to be, and it should have the overhanging sides; I've never made anything else on a regular basis."

Historically, then, traditional folk cultural forms have been conservative, resistant to change. Yet it must also be recognized that traditional folk cultural forms cannot be properly understood by positing historical "eras" or "movements" as though change came about only because of and within such theoretical frameworks, and that therefore traditional forms or styles can be traced in some sort of evolutionary succession of temporal progressive steps; such erroneous but nonetheless widespread approaches to sociocultural reality, and especially creative and artistic phenomena, simply have no bases in fact, rather seem themselves to have evolved solely from the minds of analysts; furthermore, such approaches totally ignore crucial considerations of everyday audience influence and the omnipresent personal creative and innovative nature of the craftsman or performer. Providing insightful observations and questions for folklorists, John Burrison writes:

> The role of the folk "artist" is more that of a culture-reinforcer or interpreter than of a dissenter or critic of his group's ways. The relationship between such culturally limited creativity and the existing patterns of tradition is a fascinating one and presents some important questions to the folklorist. . . . First, what categories of creativity exist in a tradition-based society? Innovation, re-creation, and individual interpretation all represent degrees of creativity, which are not confined to a

created product itself (such as a song or a chair [or a dulcimer]) but apply also to performance (the manner of presentation or delivery) and production techniques, as well as to selection of items for one's repertoire (akin to an editing or focusing process and involving aesthetic judgment).

Second, need an item, once created within a folk community, actually circulate in the community (that is, *become* traditional) to be considered folklore? . . . Cannot folklore, then, be that which arises out of tradition as well as that which has passed into tradition?

Third, how are creative processes affected when the traditional society is being overwhelmed by a larger change-directed, urban-industrial society?[57]

The responsibility of the folklorist, museum curator, and cultural interpreter is to document what changes have occurred in a traditional process and, to the extent possible, why they occurred and how and when. This I have tried to do concerning Homer Ledford's dulcimer craft.

Certainly one cannot begin to comment meaningfully on Homer's handcrafted musical instruments—from his first matchstick fiddle to the dulcimers he presently crafts to such perfection—without thoroughly appreciating all of the various influences, folkloric and nonfolkloric, upon Homer Ledford: the boy, the man, and the craftsman; and perhaps more important, the manner in which he responded to those seemingly divergent influences. Even more difficult to place in perspective are the apparently purely creative or innovative aspects of Homer's craft, such as the specialized tools he has developed and the two new instruments he has invented. The dulcitar and dulcibro represent a blending of nearly all of the influences herein discussed: folk craftsmanship, tradition, popular culture's influence, musical expertise, and—perhaps most evident—innovation. Yet are we to say that these new instruments are simply combinations of other instruments, and several known influences? This seems insufficient. The analytic and academic problems posed here are complex; for now, all we can say is that many innovative influences, both from without and from within traditional folk-culture systems, actually invigorate established folkloric patterns of behavior.

The influence of the folk schools has perhaps been much more significant both to the perpetuation of Appalachian folk traditions and to the enthusiastic revival of folk creative arts and crafts than was previously thought. Apparently the organized folk school can serve as liaison among elite, popular, and folk cultural patterns; indeed, the very existence of a successful folk school seems to serve as proof that meaningful transitions can be realized between those cultures it bridges. Certainly Homer Ledford's experiences at the John C. Campbell Folk School and Berea College are examples of the importance of such institutions for the perpetuation of folk cultural phenomena in modern times—though such institutions do usually constitute and foster revival or revitalization approaches to folkloric phenomena, and it is not always possible to distinguish between revivals and survivals of cultural traditions. However, is it not entirely possible, even probable, that some sort of personal innovation will be manifest with *either* the traditional *or* the revival folkloric phenomena in question? In fact, personal innovation and change seem to constitute the quintessence of either type of phenomena. As Ralph Rinzler says: "We cannot celebrate . . . folk traditions without acknowledging the innovative roles of institutions and individuals."[58] Homer's entire personal history and development as a folk craftsman and musician constitute eloquent testimony to the truth of Rinzler's statement. One cannot begin to appreciate Homer's craft or his craftsmanship solely on the basis of its traditionality, for I believe Homer to be an innovative and creative traditional folk craftsman without peer.

As Michael Owen Jones has noted, "Each producer is unique in his values, aspirations, abilities, and needs; all the instruments, procedures, special lore, skills, and socioeconomic arrangements required for technological processes differ from one craftsman to another. . . . Although individual discoveries and inventions at the moment of inception are not normative for other people, *they may become so for that individual who is himself relying on tradition to some extent, and his ideas may be taken as traditional by other people at some time in the future*"[italics mine].[59] Indeed, as noted elsewhere in this study, other makers have copied some of Homer's changes, thinking they were examples of the old mountain way of doing things, and thus some of Homer's changes have *become* traditional. As Thomas Munro, another observer of processes of change, innovation, and tradition (albeit from an elite cultural viewpoint), notes, "The comparatively original part of an artist's work consists, not in thinking up completely new ideas, but in working out a few variations on one or more of the styles he inherits. . . . If his contribution, large or small, is accepted and imitated, it becomes a part of a tradition. By such gradual increments the traditions of art and of civilization develop."[60]

Homer himself states that although several people have copied his dulcimers, he has never believed in copying other living maker's designs; he would rather work out improvements himself. Once I asked Homer if he was concerned that this book might open the door to more copying of his designs and procedures. He replied, "No, not really; there's so many trying to make dulcimers now and all copying one another, they're going to do it one way or the other. Besides, if they got to copying me too much, I'd just change the way I did things. . . . They can copy everyone else all they want, but I'm not going to." However, Homer related one instance of ironic similarity despite his efforts:

That's why I changed my mandolin, because I didn't want it like Gibson's. Now it has a basic Gibson body design but I changed the neck angle and how the neck sits on the body; and I changed the carving, and the arch of the top, and the pearl inlays. So I *thought* I had made it different, but you know Mike Longworth, who now works for the Martin factory in Pennsylvania, he customized a guitar one time for himself, and he used similar designs to what I used in this mandolin; well, I took those designs and . . . rescaled them for a mandolin. And you know I had no idea where Mike must have gotten his designs in the first place, but Gibson more recently came back about five years ago and made that F5 mandolin with those same basic designs on my mandolin. Now isn't that something, and after me trying so hard not to have my mandolin like Gibson's.

Homer's individualistic creative and innovative proclivities aptly confirm the relevancy of the four-step progress toward creative performance posited by Dell Hymes. In Hymes's terms, there are many repeaters (copiers) in the dulcimer craft but relatively few creative performers (innovative craftsmen); obviously, Homer must be included in Hymes's highest category of competence: creative performance of his craft.[61]

Some of Homer's earliest innovations were motivated by both aesthetic and functional considerations. He did not like the slim, very narrow dimensions of the Thomas dulcimer, the model upon which Homer's dulcimers were based. He felt that the Thomas dulcimer was excessively fragile and fragile looking, and not well balanced; and he believed that its "pinched" size was also responsible for producing a sound that, while pleasant, could be improved. Furthermore, he did not like the narrow fingerboard because he felt that it hampered noting. He especially did not like the small unattractive pin stuck in the end of the Thomas dulcimer to secure the strings. Finally, Homer's aesthetic sensitivities rebelled completely at the finish he found on the first dulcimers he saw; to paint a handmade musical instrument was completely abhorrent to him.

Consequently, Homer made various size changes in his dulcimers shortly after he began constructing them in quantity (see page 38). From the beginning, of course, Homer has always attempted to put superior finish on his dulcimers, and has never painted one. He says that his adapted replica of the Thomas dulcimer he used as a model "just looked better, felt better, and even sounded better" than the original. Homer also changed the string-holding method (fig. 17):

My first ones had an end pin; I did it just like the old way. But later that was giving me trouble because sticking out like that it would always get knocked against something and loosen the strings . . . anyway, it looked ugly. So it just occurred to me to raise the [end] block up—it seemed simple— and that is what I did. Later that block proved to be very valuable for two other reasons. First, it gives you a place to rest your hand to play tremolo music on it, or just to rest your hand and strum; and then when you put tuners on, the [end] block comes up and protects the tuners so you won't knock them out of tune.

Shortly after he made those first changes, Homer decided that he could improve the scale of the Thomas dulcimer; he was not happy with the Thomas scale because he felt that it was not exactly correct and because it could not easily be played with other instruments. Homer then devised his own scale, primarily by ear, adjusting a typical banjo scale where he felt it necessary and appropriate to the dulcimer tone and timbre.

Because of his experiments with his dulcimer scale, Homer was naturally drawn to consider possible improvements in other technical musical aspects of his dulcimer. By coincidence, at approximately this same time, a customer discussed with Homer the problem she had in adjusting her dulcimer to agree with the rather unusual pitch she preferred. Homer's attempts to solve this problem ultimately led him to experiment with the bridge. He had always made the bridge stationary, embedded in a slot in the fingerboard; but to change the pitch of his customer's dulcimer, Homer made the bridge movable, and it worked so well that he made it a standard feature, thus enabling the instrument's tuning to be adjusted to anyone's particular needs.

Kubler observes that one technical change often leads to, or at times even demands, others, in some sort of structured, often reciprocal, concatenation of alterations within the traditional format.[62] Moreover, some changes frequently require retrospective evaluation of previous or earlier similar forms. T.S. Eliot calls attention to the fact that each significant new artistic production not only expands our appreciation and comprehension of art forms but also demands that we reassess previous artworks in a new comparative framework.[63] When improvements like Homer's are made to the dulcimer, earlier dulcimers may be evaluated as less desirable within some overall comparative framework. (Of course, changes so innovative as to alter the traditionality of the very form, such as in Homer's dulcitar and dulcibro, create different evaluative frameworks.)

Homer's technical musical improvements could not have been accomplished if Homer the craftsman had not also had considerable musical expertise. Homer is occasionally amazed that some dulcimer makers do not even know how to play the dulcimer;[64] he just does not understand "how they could make a good musical instrument if they don't know anything about music, don't even play an instrument." Certainly Homer's dual expertise in handcrafts and music has contributed to his superior dulcimer.

Homer's additional changes, some musically related and others functionally or aesthetically motivated, have already been discussed: the hollow in the underside of the fingerboard that helps prevent warping; the double-string arrangement—on his four-string dulcimer—which has already become traditional;[65] his initially reluctant switch from diamond- to heart-shaped sound holes. All of these modifications were accomplished within the first five years.

Homer has made one other, relatively minor, change in design solely to satisfy his own aesthetic notions. The scroll of the Thomas dulcimer that Homer originally replicated was blocked rather than tapered, and Homer was dissatisfied with its appearance. Consequently, within a year or so of the time that he changed the dimensions of the various dulcimer components, Homer decided to taper the scroll and curve its underside to give it a more graceful contour. This reshaping brought his dulcimer more in line with what Homer very strongly felt to be a more aesthetically proper, proportionate, and pleasing musical instrument.

59. Homer at work. *Sally Weber photo*

The fact that folk craftsmen respond to, or even have, such aesthetic notions has for too long been denied. Folk artists-craftsmen differ from elite artists-craftsmen not in degree or emotional level, but rather in the kind or form of the *paradigm* of aesthetics. Supporting this contention, William R. Ferris states that the folk artist-craftsman "utilizes aesthetic theory for innovation in his work which is comparable to that of artists on other levels of society,"[66] and Michael Owen Jones notes that the "elite *concept* [italics mine] of the aesthetic may be faulty or at least not applicable cross-culturally."[67]

Aesthetic response and expression in folk-culture processes tend to be at once more abstract and more concrete than those of elite culture; elite culture's aesthetic notions tend to be systematized or even codified, while the folk-culture aesthetic is nebulous and usually discerned only in the concrete expression of folk cultural forms. If the folk aesthetic is expressed verbally, such expression is not an overtly or consciously delineated explanation; rather it is couched in relatively emotional, everyday phraseology from which one can infer the tacitly approved aesthetic. That aesthetic notions should somehow be delineated in an analytic, or calmly detached, fashion is characteristic only of elite-culture approaches. Indeed, even an elite-culture spokesman such as Munro recognizes that "aesthetics cannot get very far if it dodges the issue of explaining the emotional aspects of aesthetic experience."[68]

My experiences with Homer and other folk craftsmen clearly indicate that aesthetic notions and expression permeate folk-culture processes and experiences. For example, Homer's remarks, randomly chosen during various stages of his making or playing a dulcimer, or selecting wood for his instruments, reveal his otherwise undelineated aesthetic: "Just look at that wood; *beautiful*; redwood; expensive, too, but it'll make a beautiful dulcimer" [said while running his hand back and forth over the wood]." "It's got a nice tone, maybe one of the best I've made." "Wowee, just listen to that." "Oh, it was the worst dulcimer I ever *did* see." "When you match 'em like that, there's nothing prettier." "Why you couldn't do that; it'd just ruin the whole appearance of it."

Homer's remarks aptly illustrate Munro's observations on the manner in which aesthetic notions permeate the everyday activities of folk culture:

> In ordinary life, and in the art activities of earlier cultures, the aesthetic attitude is and was more intimately bound up . . . with daily work, practical thinking, religious and other activities. Aesthetic enjoyment was then felt more as an integral part of these other activities, especially at the completion of periods of effort and planning.
>
> Aesthetic experience may itself include some kinds of problem-solving. . . . An *artist's* [or craftsman's] attitude is not purely aesthetic, except at certain moments of quiet contemplation; he has to spend much time and energy in *practical* thinking about his own technical problems; how to manipulate his tools and materials to produce the desired effect.[69]

Munro's suggestion that mainly "earlier" cultures possessed these characteristics is somewhat misleading, for folk-culture processes or systems are not anachronisms, as many people believe; they are as contemporary as either popular or elite processes or systems, and indeed are continually being newly created. Nonetheless, Munro's comments are certainly descriptive of the aesthetic aspects of Homer's dulcimer craft, as nearly every construction procedure possesses an aesthetic dimension for Homer, which he continually manifests either through gestures or other nonverbal communication—such as smiling and nodding while running his finger along a newly carved peg—or verbally, as in his random comments above. Moreover, every change Homer has made in his dulcimer has had an aesthetic as well as a practical or functional motivation.

Nor is the folk aesthetic necessarily static; sometimes Homer has altered or even completely discarded aesthetic notions derived from his childhood and carried over into his dulcimer craft. For example, he had never considered yellow poplar "much good for anything except kindling." Then a customer asked him to make a dulcimer for her, using some antique yellow poplar. At first, Homer was quite reluctant to do so, but the customer persisted, and Homer constructed her dulcimer from yellow poplar (for the soundboard) and black walnut (for the other parts). The result amazed him; the contrast of the light-colored yellow-green poplar against the dark walnut was "simply beautiful" to him; "I was wrong about the wood," Homer said. Consequently, he initiated a series of four-string dulcimers, made of antique woods, with yellow poplar tops and black walnut bodies. He calls these his YP 1900 dulcimers, YP meaning yellow poplar and 1900 indicating that the first one he made with a yellow poplar top was the 1,900th dulcimer he had ever crafted. To date, he has constructed several hundred in the YP 1900 series.

Homer is still not completely satisfied with some of the aesthetic aspects of the instrument:

> The biggest change I would still make is to doll up the back end so it wouldn't be so blockish looking. It still bothers me. There is no easy way; it would be easy if you didn't have to worry about selling them; that always figures in, and it keeps you from doing some things you'd really like to sometimes; that's a little thorn in the side. If you change all of that, then it's going to be more expensive, considerably more expensive to round that off and change it, make an official change. . . . [the dulcibro] had a totally round back end, like the banjo is round in the back; the side continues on around without any break for the block, no outside block to break that line [fig. 9]. That, ideally, is the way I'd really like to make dulcimers, is to have the round back end; I just like the

curves much better than the squarish things. Now, I'm satisfied with my pegbox; I think I've got that pretty much worked out, and apparently it has become something of a standard because several craftsmen have done their dulcimers the same way.

Homer would also like to carve a more aesthetically pleasing scroll with figurines and the like, but because the scroll is not only functional but also already aesthetically pleasing as it is, he is reluctant to devote more time to improving it in what he considers to be a *solely* aesthetic fashion. The end block, too, is functionally quite effective as it is. Recall Homer's comment that the end block often serves as a resting place for the player's hand; that function would be impossible if Homer redesigned the block to be round and flat. In other words, Homer sometimes sacrifices his aesthetic preferences to functional service. Yet nearly every one of his practical or functional changes has also had some aesthetic dimension, either of an auditory (musical) or visual nature.

Concerning the varied abilities of artists and craftsmen, Munro again offers some trenchant observations and helpful suggestions:

> "Art ability" or "creative ability" in general is too broad and vague a phenomenon to be effectively tested. These are names for extremely diversified and variable compound abilities. But as we analyze each of these broad abstractions into more specific, component abilities, we gradually approach the level of scientific observation and experiment. We become able (a) to single out certain traits which can be objectively measured, and which may be indicators of the less accessible ones; (b) to narrow down the inaccessible ones to more specific phases, which can be investigated inductively. "Pictorial imagination" and "musical imagination" are vague ideas, but not quite as vague as "creative imagination" in general.
>
> As we analyze artistic ability into its constituent phases, we discover that many of them are not peculiar to the aesthetic arts, but are important also in science, practical affairs, and all successful cultural achievement. General intelligence, some self-control, and the will to achieve are necessary for success in any of the channels which society esteems. . . . For instance, "general intelligence" is often estimated with special reference to verbal thinking, and measured by success

in solving verbal or numerical problems. But some kinds of intelligence may be more successful in thinking musically, with auditory images and forms, or visually, with pictorial images and forms. So our conception of the supposed general, basic abilities and their measurement may have to be revised and enlarged in dealing with the arts.[70]

When Homer commented that it was difficult if not impossible for him to comprehend how some craftsmen could make dulcimers without knowing how to play one themselves he was inadvertently pointing out such craftsmen's lack of what Munro here is calling "musical imagination." In Munro's terms, Homer, as a maker of traditional folk instruments, appears to exemplify the perfect combination of both musical and pictorial imagination or auditory and visual intelligence. Homer has revealed that he instinctively understands the kinds of distinctions Munro discusses. When I asked him about the evident lack of interest among his children in carrying on his traditional craft, he replied, "No, not a one of them seems to be interested. I wish they were, especially Mark. But, you know . . . he's just got a different kind of mind. Now when it comes to anything in math, or computers even, why he's a whiz-bang; he's even got his own computer, a small one. I couldn't do that, or wouldn't want to anyway. It's born in us; some of us can do some things just as natural, and others can't do it at all." In other words, Homer was inadvertently stating that Mark has a high degree of general intelligence (he could readily manipulate math problems and comprehend computer intricacies) but apparently does not value the musical and pictorial imagination, the auditory and visual intelligence requisite in the dulcimer craft.

Over the years I have endeavored to elicit from Homer whatever commentary he could provide to shed some light on his otherwise undelineated but nonetheless obvious aesthetic perspectives. Some of his more revealing or interesting comments follow:

> I've always thought the hourglass shape was the best for the dulcimer; the others are just variations of it; the others are really more experimental. As each maker would make his own he would change it some. . . . depends on what area you're from and how many you've seen, I think. . . . Now, I've kept that decorative edge around the border of the dulcimer [purfling] just like it was on those old Thomas dulcimers; I like that; it's pretty, and just sets it off so nice. Now the

straight box-type affair—like the German zither—is still a type of dulcimer.[71] It's the same idea; someone just made it simple, and others had more ability and put more shape to it; anybody can knock a box together and put strings on it and get something right quick to play. . . . What's pretty to me, or pleasing to me, is not necessarily pleasing to someone else. . . . I had a pretty good design teacher, but you know I really didn't learn that much, only what to call things I already knew. . . . he made us design things just because of their function, so I learned what to call designing for function—what I'd been doing for a long time. . . . When I'm making a dulcimer, or any musical instrument, I try to make it to please my eye, because my eye is trained perhaps different from someone else's eye, and I can perceive things or reject things according to my eye, and hopefully it's pleasing to someone else's. . . . But of course I don't always think all that out in those terms when I'm designing something. I just say, well okay, it's going to be like this, and I do it like that, and I guess all the experience and the little bit of training I've had takes over; and it seems like for the most part it's worked out because others have liked what I've done. I remember once at a craft fair this architect came over to me and said he had been all over to craft fairs, and my dulcimer was the only one he ever saw that made any sense design-wise. Now talk about something that made me feel good, that did.

Once in the course of our discussions, Homer remembered a dulcimer he had been given to repair, the one he called "the worst dulcimer I ever *did* see":

It was made of solid cherry; it was just as clumsy as it could be; it violated every conceivable rule for design, and it violated every rule for sound—just nailed together, a maimed-up old piece of cherry. It had three strings and they were all the same gauge . . . and put in every which way, diagonal even. I had to rebuild that thing. But it just didn't sound right; if you can imagine just stretching old rusty strings over an old board— that's what it sounded like. Well, later I put on good strings, but it still didn't sound right . . . it was too thick, and they didn't want me to trim all that thick wood either 'cause I would have to take it all apart; they just wanted it restored so it could be played. Well, I think I got maybe five notes true

on it and just left the others; it was hopeless; I don't think
they were going to play it anyway. I just couldn't bring myself
to do too much with it. It was quite deep—nearly three inches deep—but it was very narrow. The scroll thing wasn't
much of a scroll at all; it was just like taking a piece of
cherry . . . and just like taking an old chopping axe and chopping out a scroll; it was drilled out with an auger; it had three
pegs but the holes weren't right and the pegs were all different
sizes and shapes. It had round sound holes, just drilled out
with an auger.

Implicit in Homer's negative comments, of course, are his notions
of what a dulcimer should be, according to both his "musical" and
"pictorial" creative and artistic imaginative projections.

Homer's "pictorial imagination" has no doubt also been primarily
responsible for the order he has brought to the procedures, both
technical and sequential, of the dulcimer craft. Through the years
Homer has slowly evolved extremely efficient procedures for making his dulcimer, owing in part to the perceptions of his "pictorial
imagination" of how the various parts of the dulcimer should fit and
in what sequence they are best put together. In other words, first in
his mind and then with his hands, Homer has gradually broken down
the dulcimer piece by piece, experimented with methods of joining
the components, and ascertained which pieces hold the most potential for problems. For example, to master the side assembly, which
has proved problematic for dulcimer makers past and present, Homer
has evolved his own unique methods, involving the choice of materials; sizing, shaping, and assembly; special tools; and a special way
to use his pocketknife. Thus he has, through analysis and experimentation, discovered the most efficient steps for both the making of the
dulcimer's separate components and their assembly sequence (as
outlined in detail in Part II).

Likewise, Homer has found that standardization of several component parts not only saves much time, thus allowing him to construct more dulcimers than old-time mountain craftsmen could do,
but also helps him to attain considerable uniformity in the quality
of his dulcimer.

In addition to improving the technical and sequential procedures
of his craft, Homer has experimented with, designed, and produced
both new and modified tools (fig. 60) by allowing his "pictorial imagination" to project what might work to solve a given problem. When
he discovered that he needed special clamps, for example, he tried

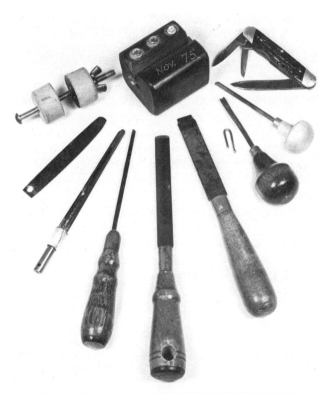

60 (*left*). Standard
hand tools
modified to
Homer's craft

61 (*below*).
Homer's
homemade pincher
clamps

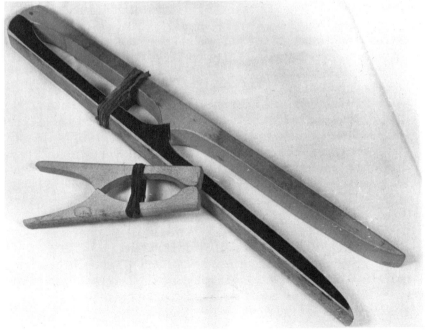

to imagine various kinds: he wanted a clamp that would hold the dulcimer top and back together without marring the wood; and he wanted the clamp to be easily manipulated and not too heavy or bulky. Again, no doubt using his "pictorial imagination" to visualize how various objects from his known environment might be altered or combined to function in the projected ideal manner, Homer finally thought of cutting up a broom handle, bolting the sections together in pairs, and lining the clamps with protective leather (page 105). Not until later did Homer discover that a very similar design was often used in violin maker's clamps.

Homer has also invented another type of clamp (fig. 61), which he uses when he does not need to be quite so careful about protecting the surface of the wood. This clamp, resembling those used on battery jumper cables, is entirely hand carved from two pieces of wood. The pieces are notched to form a fulcrum and held together with a piece of inner tube rubber, which provides the spring action. Both kinds of clamps are excellent examples of bricolage.

Another example of imagining and then constructing apparatus to achieve quality component standardization is Homer's fret maker (page 85). He projected an image of a device that would both cut the wire to exact length and bend the ends to form a staple. After experimenting with a few objects, Homer built his fret maker out of a board, an old file, some pieces of metal, a magnet, and materials to hold these items together in the proper positions (fig. 39). The device has not been altered since he first invented it; and it is an excellent example of folk-culture innovation within traditional folk cultural processes.

Homer's peg former, too (page 69) was created to achieve standardization without sacrificing the traditional handmade characteristics of dulcimer pegs. Because it was impossible to hand carve even two pegs so that they were of identical dimension, Homer attempted to visualize procedures and objects in his known environment that might apply to the problem—and soon set to work making what amounts to an oversized pencil sharpener, which is capable of tapering all of his pegs to the same thickness and slant: again, a folk-culture innovation within traditional folk cultural processes.

Two recent examples of Homer's inventory of innovative tools are the simple peg holder (page 70) that allows him to spray the tops of many pegs at once without getting lacquer on their stems; and the far more complicated frame and press for the construction of two-piece dulcimer backs (page 93). Responding to my inquiry about his source of ideas for the frame design, Homer said he "just dreamed it up," which almost is reminiscent of the contentions of other creative artists that many of their innovative ideas come from dreams or similar mental processes.[72]

Like his clamps, Homer's frame-and-press unit seems to exemplify the fact that, as Barnett observes, "all kinds of innovations can originate without their being organized by a controlling prototype."[73] The relatively new equipment replaces the makeshift apparatus Homer previously used, demonstrating that new inventions continually supplant older ones in Homer's constant endeavors to improve his craft with more efficient and effective tools and procedures.

Incisive observations concerning creative ingenuity as applied to two basic genres of innovation—artistic and utilitarian (Homer's work reflects both)—are provided by Kubler: "Useful inventions, when seen in historical sequence, show no . . . great leaps or discontinuities. Every stage follows it predecessors in a close-meshed order. Artistic inventions, however, seem to cohere by distinct levels between which the transitions are so difficult to identify that their existence may be questioned."[74] Indeed, Homer's tools, as "useful inventions," have evolved in an orderly sequence, having as their matrix the unique everyday needs of his dulcimer craft; for example, the refinement of Homer's frame and press perfectly corroborates Kubler's hypothesis, while Homer's "artistic inventions" include entirely new musical instruments, which have no discernible progression of steps, no detectable transitions between phases of development, and apparently no conceivable matrix from which they developed.

Homer's dulcitar, bicentennial dulcimer, and dulcibro—created in that order—perhaps best represent Homer's most ingenious and innovative artistic inventions. While the bicentennial dulcimer (fig. 62) is unique as a dulcimer type, it nonetheless sufficiently adheres to the traditional form to be labeled a dulcimer, but both dulcitar and dulcibro depart from any known form to the extent that they constitute entirely new instruments—having sprung from the head of Zeus, as it were.

In endeavoring to answer questions concerning his motivations for making these three unique instruments and concerning his innovative proclivities in general, Homer experienced the most difficulty; his comments were atypically brief and hesitant: "Well, it seems to me that it's just born in a person; creative urgings and so on are just part of a person. And part of it is, well, like with my uncle; he always talked about the fellow in the mountains who made the matchstick fiddle . . . well, he wanted to rise above things, to do something fantastic or outstanding, something that they would look up to." Concerning the creative impulse and its derivation from socioeconomic circumstances, Henry Glassie insightfully comments: "The notion that there is a causal relation between creativity and unconventional socioeconomic behavior is supported by the fact that the creation is often concerned with the individualistic situation— perhaps exactly that which freed the creator so that he could create or drove him to creation."[75] Homer continues: "A lot of it is curiosity, yeah. Man has always seemed to want to reach out and do something unknown, or know more about the unknown, or do something great, and I think that I just happened to be somewhat average along that line."

Because Homer's undelineated, tacitly approved, ideally amorphous aesthetic—typical of aesthetics in folk-culture processes—is inextricably bound up with and manifests itself mainly through his craft and its procedures, and because notions of innovation, creativity, and the like are in turn inextricably bound up with aesthetics, Homer finds it nearly impossible to articulate or to delineate such notions. He has such concepts; they are there; and they are intricate, complex, and sophisticated, but exist in the realm of informal, tacitly approved, unofficial, uncodified folk cultural abstractions and are embodied only in concrete folk cultural processes, designs, and forms. Consequently, Homer waxes more eloquent when he discusses a specific tangible aspect of his craft, as when he discusses the actual making of his dulcitar and dulcibro:

> It was exciting when the notion hit me that I wanted to [make the dulcitar]. One big thing that made me want to do it at that particular time, or do it at all maybe, was that I had been exhibiting various dulcimers at the Berea craftsmen's fair and I was getting kind of tired of making just dulcimers for exhibit, and I thought I wanted to do something that was different this time for people to see and, well, yeah, approval.[76] I wanted to just see if the heart-shaped body with six nylon strings on it and five chromatic frets would be good as a musical instrument, since I like music so much; but I hop from one instrument to another to play; I learn one, and get a little tired of it and want to go to something new. So this was definitely new. I just took a piece of brown paper down into the shop and took the scissors—I folded the paper, you know, so I'd have a center line—and took the scissors in order to make it symmetrical and snipped out the heart-shaped body, and that was it. I never did change it.

62. Homer's
bicentennial dulcimer

The rest of the dulcitar story has already been discussed, but certain aspects of Homer's creative process as it pertains to the dulcitar
deserve further attention. First, it is significant that Homer felt the
instrument to be a startling innovation, one that should bring him
recognition and approval; it was *his* creation. Consequently when
someone tried to pirate the dulcitar, Homer was understandably upset;
a part of him, a tangible product of his innovative, artistic ingenuity,
was being stolen. As a result of that experience, Homer subsequently patented his dulcitar, making it legally as well as creatively his.
Furthermore, Homer never intended to sell the dulcitar as he does

his other instruments; he has made only a few on special order—
twenty to date—and not only does he not want to promote the dulcitar
as he does his dulcimer, but customers apparently do not respond to
it in the same way. Both recognize that it is unique, truly a part of
Homer, hence neither to be distributed as a traditional form nor
popularized. As Barnett notes, "Some innovations are by the circumstances of their origin individualized prerogatives. They are not
intended to be popularized because they are symbols of distinction.
They put the stamp of uniqueness upon their originator and have this
function only. They are in a sense trade-marks and are valued for that
reason."[77] It is possible that in time Homer's dulcitar will itself be
considered a traditional instrument, but for the present even the
Smithsonian Institution regards it as an example of unique innovation within folk-culture processes.

It is also significant for an understanding of creative processes
that Homer reveals that the boredom of repetition in his dulcimer
craft was partly responsible for the creation of the dulcitar. Recogniz-
ing this phenomenon, Kubler comments that the "artist himself is
most exposed to tedium, overcoming it by the invention of new formal combinations and by more daring advances in previously established directions. These advances obey a rule of gradual differentiation because they must remain as recognizable variations upon the
dominant memory image."[78]

Although the dulcitar and dulcibro are unique, are creative innovations, their components are still recognizable: in the dulcitar can
be seen aspects of both the dulcimer and the guitar; in the dulcibro,
aspects of the dulcimer, the guitar, the mandolin, and the dobro; yet
all components are uniquely combined. The dulcimer, itself perhaps
a more complex form deriving from the zither family, has provided
Homer with basic ideas from which first to develop various elabora-
tions of the dulcimer—of which the Bicentennial dulcimer is one—
and then to metamorphose the dulcimer into even more complex
forms by combining its components with those of other instruments
to form unique and complex hybrids.

There is nothing new in this *process*; rather the *components*
merely change as the sociocultural milieux change in which a craftsman creates. The matchsticks Homer used to make his first fiddle
were components from other cultural systems utilized in a folk
cultural mode of production and ingenious creation. As Homer has
grown older, and as society and cultures have changed, and as Homer
has been exposed to increasingly more diverse sociocultural
phenomena, he has at his disposal more and more sources from which

to choose components for experimentation. By combining culturally diverse components, Homer not only reveals his creative ingenuity but also displays his daring and adventuresome nature, a
characteristic that is relatively rare among traditionally more conservative folk-culture artists and craftsmen. The observations of
Henry Glassie concerning performers of oral traditions can be equally applied to folk craftsmen such as Homer:

> The contemporary performer [or artist-craftsman] whose cul-
> ture includes strong folk components can choose for perfor-
> mance [or manufacture] from among a variety of models rang-
> ing from those which were archaic when he was first exposed
> to them as a child [for Homer, the Thomas dulcimer form],
> to those which were the latest ideas of our society when they
> were presented to him on television yesterday. The norm is
> to accept a whole from tradition [such as Homer's dulcimer]
> or from outside [such as Homer's banjos, guitars, fiddles, and
> mandolins]. Safe creation generally consists of innovation
> within a single model [such as Homer's innovative modifica-
> tions to his traditional dulcimer] or combination of similar
> models from the same source [such as Homer's teardrop,
> sweetheart, and Bicentennial dulcimers]. The adventurous
> creator frequently combines models selected from different
> cultural inventories [such as Homer's dulcitar and dul-
> cibro.][79]

In creating his dulcibro design, Homer employed the same technique with which he designed the form of his dulcitar:

> You know, this dulcibro was done the same way—I didn't
> change it once I clipped it out. Instead of a brown paper bag,
> I had graph paper big enough that I put two sheets together
> and folded it and made it a little easier. . . . I did take a pencil
> and make a quick outline, but I didn't follow the pencil line
> one hundred percent. I've got a knack, apparently, with us-
> ing scissors. I can design with the scissors better than I can
> with a pencil. For one of the reasons—I think it is—I carve,
> and my right wrist is so used to being controlled; when I'm
> carving on a curved piece, my wrist knows what to do after
> all that experience and so forth; at first, though, I was as
> awkward as anybody. But anyway, here I go snip, snip, snip,
> and that dulcibro just happened, just like that; and that

scroll—everybody says they just love it, and I do too—and I couldn't change it a bit, 'cause if I changed it I think it would ruin it. And how that happened I don't know exactly, unless it's just being used to my wrist making circular movements, and so forth, from my carving, and that's of course a whole lot of years of carving; your mind thinks the same thing and your hand's just doing what your mind's telling it to.

Homer's comments seem to corroborate many observers' conclusions concerning the creative act and "the necessity of conceptualizing a subject before it can be articulated [in form]." In fact, Homer's words, "your hand's just doing what your mind's telling it to," are nearly identical to those of another folk artist-craftsman, whose medium is clay, when he says: "If you ain't got it in your head, you can't do it in your hand."[80] Again, both comments reflect the fact that in folk-culture systems and processes, aesthetic notions are simultaneously abstract (in the mind or feelings, but amorphously so, not codified) and concrete (finding tangible expression only in the product rather than in some logically delineated presentation of rules, guidelines, or characteristics).

As Munro states, "The aesthetic attitude is in some ways passive and compliant, in following attentively some series of outer stimuli, rather than pursuing a spontaneous course of thought or action."[81] In other words, Homer and other folk creators express their aesthetic notions in the process of creating; such expression is a rather ordered manifestation of an otherwise unordered aesthetic; and such ordering in concrete creativity is usually the closest that the folk aesthetic comes to being presented in organized fashion. Hence, Homer cuts out his designs not haphazardly, not spontaneously, not from a dream vision, but by following the unstated guidelines of folk cultural aesthetic notions of form in his mind. Of course, Homer also has acquired notions of form, of aesthetics, and of design from popular and elite culture; and all three systems especially converge when Homer engages in the kind of innovative artistry that created his dulcitar and his dulcibro. Yet the manner in which Homer creates and the resulting form, design, and expressed aesthetic still appear to be predominantly folk cultural in nature, even though the final product is not traditional. Folk-culture predominance is also manifested in the fact that Homer feels that he must call his two newly created instruments *dulci*-tar and *dulci*-bro, indicating that they are predominantly derivatives of his traditional Appalachian dulcimer and associated folk cultural conceptions of form, design, function, and aesthetics.

When asked if he felt that his dulcitar and dulcibro were "art" or "craft" objects, Homer seemed rather puzzled. It must be remembered that originally, in the development of Western Civilization, there was no differentiation in the terms, and etymologically there is still little difference. Homer believes, however, that musical instrument making in general is a craft, but that there are aspects of the craft which could be called art, such as designing, custom carving and inlaying, and decorative features in general. Homer feels that when he actually designed the new forms of his dulcitar and dulcibro he was doing artwork, and that when he experimented with new combinations of various components of other instruments, and when he decorated the new instruments, he was engaged in artistic creativity. Yet he still feels that the actual construction of the total instruments was craftwork. Homer's views seem to bear out Jones's observations that "some evidence indicates that there is in the creation of traditional and conventionalized modes of artistic expression a manipulation of form, and even the attempt to create something that is a new combination of formal elements (an innovation), but it is difficult to find art for art's sake or the deliberate manipulation of form for its own sake."[82] Homer conceives of the making of musical instruments as a craft because the end product is predominantly functional; he simply does not conceive of the dulcimer as an art object, but rather as a useful and usable (but nonetheless beautiful) musical instrument—a craft object; hence he sees the artistic aspects of the instrument as incidental. As Homer says, only when he is "drawing to the line," or "designing new elements or shape," or "decorating" does he consider his activity "art."[83] Even art historian and philosopher Munro, who usually concerns himself more with elite culture and its artists and art forms, recognizes that "ordinarily, artists are not satisfied with purely natural or aimless products; they try to improve on nature and upon the scenes of human life, as by inventing new musical instruments and forms."[84] Munro's comments describe not only Homer's activities but also Homer's own conception of what he does.

It is always obvious that Homer thoroughly enjoys his innovative activities, and he usually has one or more exciting ideas in mind:

> I have a ball. It's when I have to make the same thing over and over that it gets dull sometimes. I want to be more creative. The trouble is I've got these orders stacked up here and it's all the same thing pretty much, only difference is the wood maybe, and that's always nice. Right now I'd like to finish Julie's fiddle [Homer was making a new fiddle for his

daughter; it was the third fiddle he had ever made], and after that I have another idea that I want to use in an instrument, a new principle. It has to do with taking a circular spruce top, roughly the same size as an 11-inch banjo head, and instead of gluing it down onto a rim like a guitar top, put it under tension with a loop that pulls that top down and puts that into a stress; then set the bridge off center. Then see what kind of sound I can get out of that, and I know it's going to sound good; it about has to, because in a sense it's using the same principle as a mandolin; you're just pressing the carved arched top down in a reverse manner; it's almost a folded speaker . . . and gives you more vibrating surface—well, it's like a diaphragm, but not completely. . . . I don't know what I'm going to call that one. . . . it is something new, something refreshing to me. I think most people feel that way, that it would be nice to have something new, something different, whether it's a song, poem, thinking, or whatever it might be—a new angle; it is a desire to create.

Homer's desire to create his Bicentennial dulcimer, however, was motivated by other than his creative muse. A customer, evidently caught up in the Bicentennial spirit, insisted that Homer construct a special dulcimer commemorating the nation's two-hundredth birthday. In creating his Bicentennial dulcimer under such circumstances, Homer was responding to what Jones identifies as "the value of uniqueness, so strongly emphasized by outsiders conditioned to constant changes in mass production and the popular [culture] arts, that serves as motivation for the traditional craftsmen to utilize their imagination in creating new designs."[85] Yet Homer, in such a situation, remains distinct from the popular-culture creator who is more or less rigidly manipulated by the mass consuming public who, in turn, are manipulated by popular-culture advertising and the like. Moreover, as stated earlier, even Homer's most innovative creations always reflect a considerable degree of traditional folk-culture form, design, aesthetics, and so on. Also, as far as I can determine, Homer has never been overly concerned with fads and fashions, nor has he been excessively affected by potential customers' ideas about what he should or should not do.[86] On occasion, however, he will yield to a request:

A friend of mine asked me to make him a Bicentennial dulcimer. At first I didn't want to; I was sick and tired of

Bicentennial this and Bicentennial that, but he kept after me, so in May [of 1976] I started to make it. I didn't know what in the world I was going to do; I didn't know what it was going to look like exactly; but I knew it had to be something "Bicentennial" looking. So I thought I would make it out of fancy wood. . . . As it turned out, I accidently found some black walnut over at Shakertown [a restored Shaker settlement near Lawrenceburg, Kentucky] which was 200 years old, so I got to put that into it too. The top was yellow poplar, old poplar, and the back was a two-piece book-matched curly walnut, and the sides were curly walnut too. I made the fingerboard [also walnut] so it had four holes in each side of it, so that they joined with the hollowed-out underside of the fingerboard to make actually eight more sound holes, four on each side of the fingerboard. How much good that has done . . . I dont' know; I never made anything like it; I think it had to help the sound some. . . .

And I had two holly inlays down each side of the fingerboard to give it a white line to kind of dress off the edges. It had four stars inlaid in the fingerboard for position markers; now on the guitar you have position markers [for musical notes] for various positions on the fingerboard, and I thought you could do that on a dulcimer, so I had four positions marked. I redesigned the scroll to . . . a modified-type scroll with a flat surface so that when you look at the dulcimer face on, the flat surface would look right at you . . . on there I put an eagle. The eagle I designed from a 1880-something silver dollar, and I cut the eagle in mother-of-pearl and set it in that flat surface. I put stars for sound holes.

I only made thirteen [Bicentennial dulcimers], but that was not intentional; I had set out to make forty of them, but time ran out. I only made them *in* 1976. And, you now, some people have told me that it's already considered a highly valuable instrument. . . . I know at least one of them has already been passed down to family; yes sir, one lady that bought one in Ohio died, and left it to her relatives.

Obviously, Homer values the fact that his Bicentennial dulcimer not only is considered valuable for its uniqueness but also reflects traditional values—both the Appalachian and the American heritage—and is itself evidently becoming a traditional object by virtue of its being passed from generation to generation.

63. Sleeve of the Ledford family record

The innovative changes Homer has introduced into the dulcimer craft are examples of how modern folk ingenuity can combine with traditional processes, thus further enhancing the products. All traditional phenomena have their origins somewhere in time and place. Simply because the time or place is known—and even if the time and place are near to us—such knowledge by itself cannot be used to disclaim an item's folkloric value; however, it is not often that opportunities are provided to document innovative folkloric developments. With such data, antiquarian-oriented demands of anonymity of origin, immutability, spatial proliferation, and longevity are not necessarily prerequisites for acceptable status as folkloric phenomena. To put it another way, Homer's peg fitter and fret maker seem not unlike the traditional pattern he uses as the basic shape of his dulcimer; the difference is that the patten is not *his* invention; its originator is anonymous. If as much were known about the pattern's inventor and the process of its invention as we know about other aspects of Homer's craft, such knowledge would not detract from its folkloric, or folkloristic, significance.

In Homer Ledford's personal history as a folk craftsman, we see a good example of how popular-culture adherents, desirous of handmade objects to satisfy folk-culture tendencies in their lives, can stimulate a revival of interest in a waning folkcraft, thus creating an increased demand for its products; as a result, an existing folk craftsman who earned his living elsewhere is able to engage in his newly viable craft as a full-time paying occupation. To do so, the craftsman first had to perfect the traditional craft through innovative methods of production, but without sacrificing any of its traditional aspects; this Homer Ledford has accomplished in ingenious fashion. In a sense, Homer's innovative approaches to dulcimer making are analogous to custom work adorning many standard traditional instruments; both are embellishments upon the traditional handicraft—one upon its procedures, the other upon its products.

Often the fusion of traditional folk-culture forms with aspects of popular and elite culture result in innovative objects lower in quality than any of the separate components; yet as Jones notes, such acculturation can also raise the quality of the products.[87] There is no doubt that in Homer's instance, creativity, innovation, and development of his talents through mild acculturation from other systems have not only perfected Homer's traditional dulcimer craft but at the same time permitted him to create intriguing new products. In all of his creative activities, Homer seems to have fulfilled every requisite Munro lists for captivating the attention of audiences for art products:

discriminate selection of forms; detachment of the form and the process of its creation from the outside world; intensification of the forms; variety and contrast; and internal organization or unity of form.[88] In each of Homer's instruments and in Homer's craft itself, these characeristics seem to be reflected and integrated to a degree of perfection not usual in other makers' dulcimers.

Homer's creativity within traditional frameworks and in the folk cultural mode is of the order described by Clark Moustakas: "Creativity is not adaptation. It always involves a solemn compact between one's self and others or between one's self and the raw materials of nature and life. It is a pure form of self-other relatedness."[89] Such is the quintessence of Homer Ledford's approach to his craft, not only in his creative and innovative endeavors but also in his simultaneous devotion to tradition. The combination produces the traditional yet unique Ledford dulcimers as well as the unique yet traditionally derived dulcitar and dulcibro, all of which evolve from an ever-changing interaction among Homer, his creative ideas, and his customers—as they all exist in a complex society whose dynamics are motivated by an intricate combination of folk, popular, and elite cultural systems and processes.

Homer's unique personal history and development as a craftsman better enable him, as he says, "to make my dulcimers to last, and I hope they will be passed on from generation to generation." Anyone who owns one of his instruments would heartily agree that in all probability Homer's wish will be realized.

NOTES

Introduction

1. That the dulcimer qualifies as a folk instrument I believe no one disputes; see Charles Seeger's definitive article, "The Appalachian Dulcimer," *Journal of American Folklore* 71 (1958): 40-51.

2. For discussions of origins, see Charles Faulkner Bryan, "American Folk Instruments: Improvised Instruments," *Tennessee Folklore Society Bulletin* 18 (September 1952): 3; Bryan, "America's Folk Instrument: The Appalachian Dulcimer," *Tennessee Folklore Society Bulletin* 18 (March 1952): 1-5; Bryan, "Appalachian Mountain Dulcimer Enigma," *Tennessee Folklore Society Bulletin* 20 (September 1954): 86-90; Allen H. Eaton, *Handicrafts of the Southern Highlands* (New York: Russell Sage Foundation, 1937), 199-204; Scott Odell, "Folk Instruments," *Arts in Virginia* 12 (Fall 1971): 30-37; Jean Ritchie, *The Dulcimer Book* (New York: Oak Publications, 1963); Seeger, 40-51; L. Allen Smith, *A Catalogue of Pre-Revival Appalachian Dulcimers* (Columbia: University of Missouri Press, 1983); L. Allen Smith, "Toward a Reconstruction of the Development of the Appalachian Dulcimer," *Journal of American Folklore* 93 (1980): 385-96; Vernon Taylor, "From Fancy to Fact in Dulcimer Discoveries," *Tennessee Folklore Society Bulletin* 23 (September 1957): 86-90.

3. For possible European antecedents, see Anthony Baines, *Musical Instruments through the Ages* (Baltimore: Penguin, 1961), 210-11; R.P. Hommel in *Antiques* 23 (December 1932): 238; Henry C. Mercer, "The Zithers of the Pennsylvania Germans," *A Collection of Papers Read Before the Bucks County Historical Society* 5 (1926): 482-97; Hortense Panum, *The Stringed Instruments of the Middle Ages: Their Evolution and Development* (London, n.d.), 263-91; Michael Praetorius, *Syntagma Musicum* (Wolffenbuttel, 1620), vol. 3; Ritchie, *Dulcimer Book*, passim.

4. For example, see Jean Ritchie, *Dulcimer People* (New York: Oak Publications, 1975), 45-51; Seeger, passim; Michael Murphy, *The Appalachian Dulcimer Book* (St. Clairsville, Ohio: The Folksay Press, 1976), passim.

5. Joseph C. Hickerson of the Library of Congress Folk Music Archive has published an excellent bibliography listing more than seventy items pertaining to the Appalachian dulcimer, but nearly all of these sources deal primarily with the craft, not the craftsmen. See his *Bibliography of Hammered and Plucked (Appalachian or Mountain) Dulcimers and Related Instruments* (Washington, D.C.: Library of Con-

gress, 1971). Even Ritchie's *Dulcimer People* provides relatively little biographical data. Many of the published materials dealing with the craftsmen are in the form of human-interest newspaper accounts. The following is just a partial list of popular or journalistic works on Homer Ledford: "City High Teacher Recognized as Outstanding Producer of Hand-Carved Music Instruments," *Winchester Sun*, 26 Jan. 1956; "Clark County Teacher to Exhibit Dulcimers at Craftsman's Show," *Smoke Signals* (Clark County, Kentucky, High School), 20 Oct. 1961; Paul Deutschman, "Rebirth in the Hollers," *Travel and Camera*, Sept. 1969, 62-67; "Dulcimer-Maker Plans Exhibit," *Winchester Sun*, 3 Oct. 1961; "Dulcimers' Twang Heard at Eastern," *Louisville Courier-Journal*, 5 July 1963; Edward L. Dupuy, *Artisans of the Appalachians* (Asheville, N.C.: Miller Printing Company, 1967), 74; John Fetterman, "An Overton County Dulcimer Builder," *Nashville Tennessean Magazine*, 30 May 1954, 8; "Handicapped Mountain Boy Finds Genius in Woodcraft," *Nashville Banner*, 23 Aug. 1951; *The Hills Resound—The Music of Kentucky*, TV film, Kentucky Authority for Educational Television; "I.A. Student Is Instrument Maker," *Eastern Progress* (Eastern Kentucky State Teachers College), 19 Jan. 1953; "Numerous Activities Being Planned for Third Kentucky Folk Festival," *Lexington Herald-Leader* 5 April 1953; "Skilled Craftsmen of the Southern Highlands Show Wares," *Greenville News*, 27 July 1952; "Southern Appalachian Folk Pursue Old Craft Skills to Lift Incomes," *Wall Street Journal*, 18 Dec. 1961; "These Two Crafts-men Have Turned Out 250 Dulcimers," *Courier-Journal and Louisville Times Sunday Magazine*, 20 Jan. 1952, 27-28; Ruth Walker, "Fifth Annual Fair Staged in Asheville," *Greenville News*, 26 July 1952.

6. John F. Putnam, *The Plucked Dulcimer* (Berea, Ky.: The Council of the Southern Mountains, 1964), 7; Ralph Rinzler, Introduction, *1973 Festival of American Folklife* (Washington, D.C.: Smithsonian Institution, 1973), 2.

7. Michael Owen Jones, *The Hand Made Object and Its Maker* (Los Angeles: University of California Press, 1975), vi-vii. To illustrate the trend in folkloristics for more biographical-psychological studies, see also Roger D. Abrahams, ed., *A Singer and Her Songs: Almeda Riddle's Book of Ballads* (Baton Rouge: Louisiana State University Press, 1970); Henry Glassie et al., eds., *Folksongs and Their Makers* (Bowling Green, Ohio: Bowling Green University Popular Press, 1970); Glassie, "Take that Night Train to Selma: An Excursion to the Outskirts of Scholarship," *Journal of Popular Culture* 2 (Summer 1968): 1-62; Edward D. Ives, *Joe Scott, The Woodsman-Songmaker* (Urbana: University of Illinois Press, 1978); Ives, *Larry Gorman: The Man Who Made the Songs* (Bloomington: Indiana University Press, 1964); Leonard Roberts, *Sang Branch Settlers* (Austin: University of Texas Press, 1974); Ellen J. Stekert, "Two Voices of Tradition" (Ph.D. diss., University of Pennsylvania, 1965). See also the several articles in John A. Burrison, ed., *Creativity in Southern Folklore, Studies in the Literary Imagination* (special edition) 3 (April 1970). It should be apparent that nearly all of these works deal with other than folk craftsmen or artists, indicating a scholarly lacuna that has existed for a long while.

8. Burrison, 1.

9. Ives, *Joe Scott*, xii-xiv.

10. Homer Garner Barnett, *Innovation: The Basis of Cultural Change* (New York: McGraw-Hill, 1953), 379ff.; cf. Barnett's discussion of "cultural predisposition," 39-40.

11. Ferris's work is reflected in his article " 'If you Ain't Got It in Your Head, You Can't Do It in Your Hand': James Thomas, Mississippi Delta Folk Sculptor," in Burrison, 89-107; Joyner's excellent but brief study is "Dulcimer Making in Western North Carolina: Creativity in a Traditional Mountain Craft," *Southern Folklore Quarterly* 39 (1975): 341-61; the others have already been cited.

12. Michael Owen Jones's suggested guidelines for pursuing research on traditional furniture are excellent, and many of his perspectives agree with those I used in this study; see "The Study of Traditional Furniture: Review and Preview," *Keystone Folklore Quarterly* 12 (Winter 1967): 233-46. See also M.O. Jones, "Two Directions for Folkloristics in the Study of American Art," *Southern Folklore Quarterly* 32 (1968): 249-59.

13. For a guide to the Smithsonian's dulcimer collection, see Scott Odell, *Plucked Dulcimers: A Checklist of Appalachian Dulcimers and Similar Instruments in the Collections of the Division of Musical Instruments, Smithsonian Institution* (Washington, D.C.: Smithsonian Institution, n.d.).

14. See Michael Owen Jones's comment on this topic in "Folk Art Production and the Folklorist's Obligation," *Journal of Popular Culture* 4 (1970): 194-212.

15. James V. Kavanaugh, "The Artifact in American Culture: The Development of an Undergraduate Program in American Studies," in *Material Culture and the Study of American Life*, ed. Ian M.G. Quimby (New York: W.W. Norton and Company, 1978), 68. For general discussions concerning the place of folklife studies in the understanding of American life, consult Ward H. Goodenough, "Folklife Study and Social Change," and Don Yoder, "Folklife Studies in American Scholarship," both in *American Folklife*, ed. Don Yoder (Austin: University of Texas Press, 1976); especially see Yoder's bibliography. See also Norbert F. Riedl, "Folklore and the Study of Material Aspects of Folk Culture," *Journal of American Folklife* 79 (1966): 557-63; Don Yoder, "The Folklife Studies Movement," *Pennsylvania Folklife* 13 (July 1963): 43-56.

I: HOMER LEDFORD: THE MAN AND THE CRAFTSMAN

1. Play-parties were affairs allowing the sexes to mix. They usually involved music and nontouching dancing, and thus did not break religious taboos. For illustrative data on such activities, see W. Edson Richmond and William Tillson, "The Play Party in Indiana," *Indiana Historical Society Publications* 20 (1959): 103-326; B.A. Botkin, *The American Play-Party Song* (Lincoln: University of Nebraska Press, 1937); Horace Kephart, *Our Southern Highlanders* (Knoxville: University of Tennessee Press, 1976), 338. Buck-wing, or buck and wing, dancing is primarily a solo dance style, though several people may do it at the same time; see Walter G. Raffe, comp., *Dictionary of the Dance* (New York: A.S. Barnes, 1964), 79.

2. Homer is uncertain of the title of this songbook, but believes it may have been *Songs of All Time* (Berea, Ky.: Council of Southern Mountain Workers, 1946).

3. This characteristic is well documented; for example, see John C. Campbell, *The Southern Highlander and His Homeland* (Lexington: University Press of Kentucky, 1969), 93, 300, et passim; Kephart, 280-81, 288, 328-29, 393-94; James Watt Raine, *The Land of Saddle-bags* (New York: Council of Women for Home Missions, 1924), 69, 74-75, 85; and the controversial modern work, Jack E. Weller, *Yesterday's People* (Lexington: University Press of Kentucky, 1965), 31-33, 48, 102, and the Appendix (163), where his trait number 33 is "suspicion and fear of outside world." For somewhat different views of some topics Weller discusses, see Stephen L. Fisher, "Victim-Blaming in Appalachia: Cultural Theories and the Southern Mountaineer," in *Appalachia: Social Context Past and Present*, ed. Bruce Ergood and Bruce E. Kuhre (Dubuque: Kendall-Hunt, 1978), 139-48; Loyal Jones, "Appalachian Values," in *Voices from the Hills: Selected Readings of Southern Appalachia*, ed. Robert J. Higgs and Ambrose N. Manning (New York: Frederick Ungar, 1975), 507-17.

4. Homer does not disparage any music simply because it happens to be in print;

indeed, he believes that print actually serves to perpetuate the old-time songs.

5. For a fine discussion of C.W. von Sydow's distinction of "active/passive" repertoire items, see Kenneth S. Goldstein, "On the Application of the Concepts of Active and Inactive Traditions to the Study of Repertory," *Journal of American Folklore* 84 (1971): 62-67. My data on the community of Homer's youth seem to support the contention that an item may very well be known, even by heart, but not ever performed; in this case, suppression appears to have been the result primarily of an overriding preference for religious music.

6. D.K. Wilgus and Archie Green have been perhaps the two strongest proponents of the need to analyze the inter-relationships of mass communication media and folkloric phenomena; their tenets are familiar to all folklorists. Many of their postulations seem to be well illustrated in my data on Homer Ledford. See especially Wilgus's two contributions to the Hillbilly Issue of *Journal of American Folklore* 78 (1965): "An Introduction to the Study of Hillbilly Music," 195-203; "Current Hillbilly Recordings: A Review Article," 267-287. His "Country-Western Music and the Urban Hillbilly," *Journal of American Folklore*, 83 (1970): 157-79, also discusses intercultural influences and mass media. Archie Green's *Only a Miner: Studies in Recorded Coal-Mining Songs* (Urbana: University of Illinois Press, 1972), passim, is perhaps his most eloquent commentary on this topic.

7. Before he died, Buell Kazee had made his home in Winchester, Kentucky, the same town in which Homer and I now reside; over the years, the two men naturally became good friends. I have a tape recording of Kazee (possibly the last one made) singing and playing the banjo at Homer's home. For more information on Kazee see Archie Green's book cited above.

8. See Green's and Wilgus's works, cited in note 6, for a discussion of the characteristics of these musical styles. See also L. Mayne Smith, "An Introduction to Bluegrass," *Journal of American Folklore* 78 (1965): 245-56. Homer himself is extremely knowledgeable and articulate concerning various musical styles.

9. Wilgus, "Current Hillbilly Recordings," 271.

10. See Green, passim, especially 58, 59, 447.

11. Quoted from the dust jacket of Green's *Only a Miner*.

12. Green, 58, 59, 447.

13. Homer has produced an LP recording which presents several of these instruments played by him and some of his children: *The Ledford Family: Songs We Love to Sing and Play* (RCM S012050, S012051) (fig. 63, page 168).

14. Shape notes were simply different figures—a square, a diamond, a triangle, and so forth—used to designate the different notes on the musical scale; each note could easily be memorized by associating it with its distinctive shape. Homer cannot recall the name of the particular shape note songbook his uncle used, but he is certain that it employed the seven-shape system. For information on the shape note tradition, see George Pullen Jackson, *White Spirituals in the Southern Uplands* (Hatboro, Pa.: Folklore Associates, 1964).

15. This is the hymn Jackson includes as number six in his list of "Eighty Most Popular Tunes," 134.

16. J.C. Campbell, 93.

17. Pat McNelley, ed., *The First 40 Years: John C. Campbell Folk School* (Atlanta: McNelley-Rudd Printing Service, 1966), 14.

18. John C. Campbell died in 1919; Olive Dame Campbell died in 1954.

19. Olive D. Campbell, "Are We Developing Dependence or Independence?," in *Mountain Life and Work* (1928), 10.

20. Now Edna Ritchie Baker, this remarkable woman and her husband, Floyd Baker, for years not only accompanied Homer's performances but frequently appeared on the same program as performers in their own right. The Bakers' music is included in Homer's album, referred to in note 13 above. Edna continues to reside in Winchester, Kentucky. For information on Edna and the Ritchie family, consult Ritchie, *Dulcimer People*; Ritchie, *Singing Family of the Cumberlands* (New York: Oxford University Press, 1957); Edna's recording, *Edna Ritchie of Viper, Kentucky* (Sharon, Conn.: Folk-Legacy Records FSA-3).

21. Homer is not certain where this instrument is now; hence no picture or further information is available.

22. Mr. Amburgey, who died in December 1971, made dulcimers for many years. See Mildred Davidson Creighton, "Jethro Amburgey," *The Appalachian South* 1 (Summer 1965): 24-25. The *Courier-Journal and Louisville Times Sunday Magazine* once printed two juxtaposed articles, one on Homer and the other on Jethro; see "These Two Craftsmen Have Turned out 250 Dulcimers" (cited in note 5 of the Introduction).

23. Seeger, 40. Seeger also includes Homer in his list of traditional dulcimer craftsmen (51, note 16).

24. Quoted in Seeger, 44. Maud Karpeles worked with the British folksong collector, Cecil Sharp, in Appalachia in the 1920's. For information on their activities, see Maud Karpeles and Arthur Henry Fox-Strangeways, *Cecil Sharp* (London: Oxford University Press, 1955); Cecil Sharp and Olive Dame Campbell, eds. *English Folksongs from the Southern Appalachians* (London: Oxford University Press, 1917).

25. J.C. Campbell, 143-44; see also Henry Glassie, *Pattern in the Material Folk Culture of the Eastern United States* (Philadephia: University of Pennsylvania Press, 1968), 84, where his dulcimer makers use a Kentucky model. There has been some speculation that the dulcimer had roots also in midwestern states such as Ohio; see Ray M. Lawless, *Folksingers and Folksongs in America* (New York: Sloan and Pearce, 1965), 261; Odell, "Folk Instruments," 30-37. However, Ohio and other highly industrialized states have long been economic meccas for many southern Highlanders; Appalachians moving to areas in the North would naturally carry their traditions with them.

26. Berea College is a self-help institution that encourages the development of handicrafts indigenous to the mountain areas it principally serves. Nearly all of Berea's students participate in the college's crafts projects; such work is accepted in lieu of a portion of a student's tuition and fees. For information on Berea College's activities, consult Elisabeth S. Peck, *Berea's First 125 Years: 1855-1980* (Lexington: University Press of Kentucky, 1982).

27. All four of the Ledford children display some of their parents' artistic abilities; all play, to some extent, at least one musical instrument. Cindy, age 24, and Julie, age 22, accompanied Homer on his album (see note 13). Mattie Lee, age 18, is still too young to have developed her skills extensively, but she does play the piano and the cello. In addition, Mark, age 28, is adept at the skills of a draftsman; and Cindy has already distinguished herself as an artist of considerable talent: the sketches in this volume are Cindy Ledford's, and I deeply appreciate her time and effort in producing them.

28. This institution has expanded enormously and is now Eastern Kentucky University.

29. Dell Hymes, "Breakthrough into Performance," in *Folklore: Performance and Communication*, ed. Dan Ben-Amos and Kenneth S. Goldstein (The Hague: Mouton, 1975), 11-20. Hymes's categories and concepts are primarily meant to deal with

linguistic phenomena, but I feel they can also serve to elucidate nonverbal data.

30. Seeger, passim.

31. As will be evident, much of the following consists of Homer Ledford's own words, for who can be more eloquent in describing aspects of a handicraft than the craftsman himself? "The artists and craftsmen speak for the meaning and for the product of their skills," (Rinzler, 2), and Homer is one of those from a culture composed of "people who know who they are and where they came from," of whom Smithsonian head S. Dillon Ripley speaks in "The Festival—A Living Museum," in *1973 Festival of American Folklife* (Washington, D.C.: Smithsonian Institution), 4.

32. Among others, the McClain Family Band and Lilly May Pennington use Homer's instruments regularly.

33. Hank Levin, "How to Make an Appalachian Dulcimer," *1973 Festival of American Folklife*, 47; see also Levin's comments in Ritchie, *Dulcimer People*, 106-120.

34. The kind of aesthetic satisfaction that Homer derives from his craft is, as M.O. Jones says, "one of the essential features of folk art . . . the artistic pleasure derived from control over tools and techniques and the mastery of form, and the aesthetic pleasure derived from an involvement with and the enjoyment of form." See Michael Owen Jones, "The Concept of 'Aesthetic' in the Traditional Arts," *Western Folklore* 30 (April 1971): 93.

35. Levin, 47.

36. Several writers have dealt with the folk revival movement, especially folk song revival in urban areas. See David A. De Turk and A. Poulin, Jr., eds., *The American Folk Scene: Dimensions of the Folksong Revival* (New York: Dell, 1967), especially 13-100, 280-331; R. Serge Denisoff, *Great Day Coming: Folk Music and the American Left* (Urbana: University of Illinois Press, 1971); John Greenway, "Folklore and the Big Money," in *Our Living Traditions*, ed. Tristram P. Coffin (New York: Basic Books, 1968), 283-91.

37. Ritchie, *Dulcimer People*, 16-17. See also Eaton, 199-204, who calls Thomas "the most outstanding dulcimer maker of the Highlands" (202).

38. For a listing of basic dulcimer shapes, see Odell, *Plucked Dulcimers*, and Ritchie, *Dulcimer Book*, passim. The Thomas, and Ledford, dulcimer shape is Odell's No. 2. A fine detailing of the construction characteristics of the Thomas dulcimer is provided by S.E. Hastings, Jr., "Construction Techniques in an Old Appalachian Mountain Dulcimer," *Journal of American Folklore* 83 (1970): 462-68; the measurements of Homer's dulcimer differ only slightly from the Thomas dulcimer described by Hastings.

39. Ritchie, *Dulcimer Book*, passim.

40. These characteristics are well documented; for example, see J.C. Campbell, 8, 18, 20, 72, 88, 90-122, 178-88; Kephart, 327-28, 379-83, 455; Raine, 69-71, 73, 77, 85; Loyal Jones, 509-10.

41. Jesse Stuart, *The Thread That Runs So True* (New York: Scribner, 1958).

42. Homer made a customized dulcimer with diamond-shaped sound holes for my wife and me in 1971; it has fine border etchings, four mother-of-pearl inlays on the fingerboard, and a silver nameplate with a personal statement on the back of the pegbox; none of this changes the traditional aspects of the dulcimer itself. Also see the sketch on page 24, which represents the fine custom dulcimer Homer made for his wife.

43. D.K. Wilgus, "The Text Is the Thing," *Journal of American Folklore* 86 (1973): 245.

44. For further information on the dobro, see Kristin Baggelaar and Donald Milton,

Folk Music: More Than a Song (New York: Crowell, 1976), 105; Russ Hooper and Randy Slocum, "The Dobro Guitar and Bluegrass," *Bluegrass Unlimited* 1 (May 1967): 2-4; Bill C. Malone, *Country Music U.S.A.: A Fifty-Year History* (Austin: University of Texas Press, 1968), 123, 169, 204, 322; Irwin Stambler and Grelun Landon, *Encyclopedia of Folk, Country, and Western Music* (New York: St. Martin's, 1969), 82.

III: THE LEDFORD DULCIMER IN CONTEXT

1. For examples of folklorists' general use of the concepts, see Jan Harold Brunvand, *The Study of American Folklore: An Introduction* (New York: Norton, 1978), 2-4; Tristram P. Coffin and Hennig Cohen, eds., *Folklore in America* (Garden City, NY: Doubleday, 1966), xiii-xxi; Richard S. and A. Laurna Tallman, *Country Folks: A Handbook for Student Folklore Collectors* (Batesville: Arkansas College Folklore Archives Publications, 1978), 16-18. For popular-culture scholars' use of the concepts, see George H. Lewis, comp., *Side-Saddle on the Golden Calf: Social Structure and Popular Culture in America* (Pacific Palisades, Caliornia: Goodyear, 1972), 2-20, et passim; Russel Blaine Nye, *The Unembarrassed Muse: The Popular Arts in America* (New York: Dial, 1970). For a discussion of the influence of popular culture upon material forms of folk culture, see Glassie, *Material Folk Culture*, 17-33, et passim; for a theoretical discussion, see Glassie, "Artifacts: Folk, Popular, Imaginary, and Real," in *Icons of Popular Culture*, ed. Ray S. Browne and Marshall Fishwick (Bowling Green, Ohio: Bowling Green University Popular Press, 1970), 103-22.

2. A succinct delineation of the characteristics of popular and elite culture is provided by Russel B. Nye in his pamphlet *Notes on a Rationale for Popular Culture*, (Bowling Green, Ohio: Popular Culture Association, n.d.); however, Nye's conception of folk culture seems in error in several respects, so the characteristics of folk culture I provide herein, together with Nye's views of popular and elite culture, should provide adequate guidelines. Because one's own culture is largely out of one's awareness, but nonetheless operative, culture is rather like the nose on your face: it is always there and functional, yet one is usually unaware of it; and certainly it is impossible to see all of it clearly at one time, or as others see it.

3. Robert A. Georges, "Toward an Understanding of Storytelling Events," *Journal of American Folklore* 82 (1969): 313-28. See also Dan Ben-Amos, "Toward a Componential Model of Folklore Analysis," *Proceedings of the VIIIth International Congress of Anthropological and Ethnological Sciences* (Tokyo, 1968), 309-10; Ben-Amos, "Toward a Definition of Folklore in Context," *Journal of American Folklore* 84 (1971): 3-15. For applications of these concepts, see the several studies in Ben-Amos and Goldstein, *Folklore*; for a discussion of these folkloristic paradigms as they apply to material culture, see M.O.Jones, *Hand Made Object*, 12-25, et passim. For a contrary view, see Wilgus, "Text Is the Thing," 241-52.

4. Robert Penn Warren, "Some Don'ts for Literary Regionalists," in *Voices from the Hills: Selected Readings of Southern Appalachia*, ed. Robert J. Higgs and Ambrose N. Manning (New York: Frederick Ungar, 1975), 363.

5. For a good discussion of this long-lived folk culture form, see Duncan Emrich, *Folklore on the American Land* (Boston: Little, Brown, 1972), 205-208.

6. See D.K. Wilgus, *Anglo-American Folksong Scholarship since 1898* (New Brunswick, N.J.: Rutgers University Press, 1959), 69, 71-72, 78, 97-98, 118-120, 284, for a discussion of Barry's use of the term "communal re-creation" and its significance for folkloristics; it is now nearly a commonplace among folklorists.

7. Mitchell A. Wilder and Edgar Breitenback, *Santos: The Religious Folk Art*

of New Mexico (New York: Hacker Art Books, 1976 [c1943]). For a more recent discussion of variation within tradition and associated problems of appropriateness—which could create new versions—context, audience, and so forth, see Abrahams, 152-58; for a more philosophical approach, see George Kubler, *The Shape of Time* (New Haven: Yale University Press, 1962), 72. Kubler states: "No act ever is completely novel, and no act can ever be quite accomplished without variation."

8. See Odell, *Plucked Dulcimers;* Glassie, *Material Folk Culture,* 79-86; Chet Hines, *How to Make and Play the Dulcimore* (Harrisburg, Pa.: Stackpole, 1973), 31-54; Ritchie, *Dulcimer People,* passim; Ritchie, *Dulcimer Book,* passim.

9. See Kubler, 38-39, 101, et passim.

10. Brunvand, 2-4; Coffin and Cohen, xiii. See also Ray B. Browne, "Popular Culture: Notes toward a Definition," in Lewis, *Side-Saddle,* 5-13; Russel B. Nye, "Notes on Popular Culture," in Lewis, *Side-Saddle,* 13-20. Browne, Lewis, and Nye suggest that instead of an evolutionary scheme of "levels" of culture, the systems should be represented by a "flattened ellipsis"—thus implying not a good-better-best scheme, but just difference; such a scheme also would allow for a more accurate depiction of the diffusion that exists between the systems. For several years I have been using a parabola in a similar way to illustrate to students the relationships among the three cultural systems.

11. For good discussions of the relationships of popular and elite culture with folk culture arts and crafts, see Michael Owen Jones, "'There's Gotta Be New Designs Once in Awhile': Culture Change and the 'Folk' Arts," *Southern Folklore Quarterly* 36 (March 1972): 43-60; Joyner, 341-61. See also Jones, "Chairmaking in Appalachia: A Study of Style and Creative Imagination in American Folk Art," (Ph.D. diss., Indiana University, 1969); Jones, *Hand Made Object.* See also Glassie, "Artifacts," 106: "Folk ideas from which folk artifacts flow through manual action have been constantly influenced by popular culture."

12. For example, see Robert Redfield's classic study of cultural interrelationships: *Peasant Society and Culture: An Anthropological Approach to Civilization* (Chicago: University of Chicago Press, 1956). Redfield perhaps is the strongest early proponent of the view that cultures do not exist in isolation—what I call "under glass"—but rather that contact and tension indeed help to define different cultures; my view differs markedly in that I do not consider modern societies or cultures as isolated as those analyzed by Redfield. Joyner, 341-42, 359, accurately notes that Erikson discusses the tension of what he sees as cultural "polarities," and their effect on folk-culture processes; see Erik H. Erikson, *Childhood and Society* (Chicago: Norton, 1963), 285-87. See also the following for their comments on the absence of cultural "purity:" Jones, "There's Gotta Be New Designs"; Burrison, 1-3; Kubler, 62-82, et passim.

13. Some of these basic folkloristic concepts are discussed by Wm. Hugh Jansen, "Classifying Performance in the Study of Verbal Folklore," in *Studies in Folklore in Honor of Distinguished Service Professor Stith Thompson* (Bloomington: Indiana University Publication, 1957), 110-118; Alan Dundes, "Texture, Text, and Context," *Southern Folklore Quarterly* 28 (1964): 251-65; William R. Bascom, "Four Functions of Folklore," *Journal of American Folklore* 67 (1954): 333-49. I have altered and expanded somewhat these conceptions as I use them herein and have added others. Also, the cited scholars do not discuss these concepts in any holistic manner. It seems to me that folkloristics, with its emphasis upon folklore as communication in context, has grown out of such early discussions as those cited; yet folkloristics does not systematically use the eight components listed, either in its jargon or in research, though mention is made of these earlier studies. For example, see Ben-Amos and Goldstein,

1-7, et passim; Barre Toelken, *The Dynamics of Folklore* (Boston: Houghton Mifflin, 1979), 19-20, et passim.

14. For a fine discussion of the basic tenets of structuralism, see Jean Piaget, *Structuralism* (New York: Basic Books, 1970), 3-16, 74-143. See also Kubler, passim, for quasi-structural views of seriation and sequential replication.

15. *World of Crafts* Woodcraft Collection Catalog, January 1979, 18.

16. For example, see all the old dulcimers illustrated in Hines, 31-54; Odell, "Folk Instruments," 30, 32. See also Murphy, passim, and L.A. Smith, *A Catalogue*.

17. Originally, of course, at least the banjo was a folk instrument; the prototype is thought to have been brought to this country from Africa by slaves. However, few banjos today are created in what could be called a folk cultural process. The guitar and mandolin are not usually considered folk craft products in this country, though many have been produced in a folk cultural process: Homer has made not only banjos but guitars and mandolins as well.

18. For example, see Odell, "Folk Instruments," 36.

19. Richard M. Dorson, "Folklore and Fakelore," *American Mercury* 70 (March 1950): 335-43; Tom E. Sullenberger, "Ajax Meets the Jolly Green Giant," *Journal of American Folklore* 87 (January-March 1974): 53-65. The term was coined by Priscilla Denby, "Folklore in the Mass Media," *Folklore Forum* 4 (September 1971): 113-21. Anthropologists also discuss ersatz phenomena; for example, Barnett, 269-70.

20. See Michael Owen Jones, "A Traditional Chairmaker at Work," *Mountain Life and Work* 43 (Spring 1967): 10-13; Jones, "Study of Traditional Furniture," 233-46.

21. See Glassie's discussion of Jones's data in *Material Folk Culture*, 6-7.

22. See note 6, Part I; see also Wilgus, *Anglo-American Folksong Scholarship*, 233, for a discussion of Buell Kazee and his influence on audiences through recorded or live radio performances—a "commercialized tradition."

23. Kubler, 71; see also Kubler, 62-63, 73-74, 78, et passim, for further comments on this topic of replication and copying.

24. Brunvand, 6-7; see also Alan Dundes, ed., *The Study of Folklore* (Englewood Cliffs, N.J.: Prentice-Hall, 1965), 1-3.

25. Kubler, 76; compare M.O. Jones's similar observation ("There's Gotta Be New Designs," 59) that our modern complex society often creates paradoxical situations where quality may improve because of elite- and popular-culture influences—and because of fewer craftsmen—or may deteriorate if too many people try to capitalize on the demand for traditional objects.

26. Glassie, *Material Folk Culture*, 17, 25.

27. For information on revitalization movements, see Hadley Cantril, *The Psychology of Social Movements* (New York: John Wiley, 1941); Ward Hunt Goodenough, *Cooperation in Change* (New York: Russell Sage Foundation, 1963); Anthony F.C. Wallace, "Revitalization Movements," *American Anthropologist* 58 (1956): 264-81 (Wallace coined the term). See also the selected bibliography in Eaton; several references in Eaton's list deal with very early "revival" or even "revitalization" approaches to mountain crafts.

28. Ritchie, *Dulcimer People*, 30.

29. For information on Thomas, see the references cited in note 38, Part I.

30. See Hastings, 462-68, for an illustrated discussion of the Thomas dulcimer's construction.

31. See Henry Glassie, "Folk Art," in *Folklore and Folklife: An Introduction*, ed. Richard M. Dorson (Chicago: University of Chicago Press, 1972), 259-60 for a discussion of Levi-Strauss's term as it pertains to folkloristics. See also Claude Levi-Strauss's

original conception of bricolage in *The Savage Mind* (Chicago: University of Chicago Press, 1969), 16-22; Barnett's discussion (181-88) of the recombination of components of configurations.

32. Thomas Munro, *The Arts and Their Interrelations* (New York: Liberal Arts Press, 1949), 342.

33. Thomas Munro, *Form and Style in the Arts: An Introduction to Aesthetic Morphology* (Cleveland: Press of Case Western Reserve University, 1970), 24.

34. See the discussions of these older notions of folk culture in M.O. Jones, *Hand Made Object* 13-25, 66-82, 202-242; M.O. Jones, "There's Gotta Be New Designs;" and Joyner. For two quite different perspectives on folklore as "thing," see Burrison, 1-3; Wilgus, "Text is the Thing," passim. See also the five essays in Burrison.

35. M.O. Jones, "There's Gotta Be New Designs," 44, 52; see also M.O. Jones, "Folk Art Production," 201-2, 205-7.

36. Joyner, 345.

37. Munro, *Form and Style*, 9-10. It should be pointed out that because he makes musical instruments, Homer's work qualifies as "art" in Munro's appraisal and is listed as No. 63—"musical instrument-making"—in Munro's compilation of "one hundred visual and auditory arts;" see Munro, *Arts and Their Interrelations*, 139-42.

38. For example, see M.O. Jones's comments about nonfolk commercial markets in "Folk Art Production," 202-3, and also note Jones's reference to Glassie's remarks.

39. Kubler, 67, 130, et passim. Kavanaugh (67) states the same concept a little differently, though he is apparently influenced by Kubler: "The deep structure of the conceptual model is embodied in the artifact whatever surface form the artifact assumes."

40. M.O. Jones, "Concept of 'Aesthetic'", 94. Note also Glassie, "Artifacts," 111: "Although often treated as art, most folk material is only secondarily aesthetic in intent and function; it is craft." Jones elsewhere states that "much of art is made for active use rather than passive contemplation;" see Michael Owen Jones, "Violations of Standards of Excellence and Preference in Utilitarian Art," *Western Folklore* 32 (1973): 22, et passim.

41. See Kubler's comments (62-77, 123-27, et passim) on inventions, creative processes, and the like.

42. M.O. Jones, *Hand Made Object*, 237.

43. Joyner, 344.

44. Irving Sloane, *Making Musical Instruments* (New York: Dutton, 1978), 86.

45. Loyal Jones, 86.

46. C. Wright Mills, "The Cultural Apparatus," in *Power, Politics and People*, ed. Irving Louis Horowitz (New York: Oxford University Press, 1963), 419.

47. Munro, *Form and Style*, 10.

48. As one Appalachian scholar asserts: "A frontier farmer in the mountains was no more isolated in reference to markets than the settler in any other wilderness clearing": Cratis D. Williams,"Who Are the Southern Mountaineers?" *Appalachian Journal* 1 (Autumn 1972): 48. See also Higgs and Manning, 3-76, et passim, for early travel accounts; if there was any sort of "isolation" it was not geographic, but a preferred, self-imposed, cultural isolation.

49. M.O. Jones, *Hand Made Object*, 200.

50. M.O. Jones, "There's Gotta Be New Designs," 54-55.

51. Loyal Jones, 90.

52. M.O. Jones, "There's Gotta Be New Designs," 44.

53. Of course, all of Michael Owen Jones's works deal with innovation, change,

creativity, and so on. See also comments by Scott Odell of the Smithsonian's Division of Musical Instruments: "Strong traditions, such as the making of homemade music and musical instruments, may be reshaped by outside influences. . . . Today we are witnessing . . . an acceleration of the process of invention and change," ("Folk Instruments," 37).

54. See M.O. Jones, *Hand Made Object*, 66, 70-72, 107, 226, 250-51, 259, et passim.

55. Glassie, *Material Folk Culture*, 8. For general comments on variation within traditionally stable forms, see Brunvand, 5-7, 185-86, 200; see also Emrich's discussion of "eeny meeny miny mo" (205-208); see also Glassie's article in Brunvand, 391-420; Barnett, 49, who points out that "reproductive variation occurs in all aspects of culture. . . . It appears in handicraft."

56. Joyner, 342.

57. Burrison, 2. Glassie ("Take That Night Train to Selma," 40) notes that "creativity is frequently a byproduct of the collision of cultures."

58. Rinzler, 10.

59. M.O. Jones, *Hand Made Object*, 70, 72.

60. Munro, *Arts and Their Interrelations*, 342.

61. See my previous discussion of Hymes's concepts (pages 26-27) in Part I, as they are pertinent to an evaluation of Homer's craft. M.O. Jones ("Violations of Standards," 19) suggests that when the term "creativity" is applied to folk culture objects, it presupposes a conscious awareness of aesthetic principles.

62. Kubler, 47-48.

63. T.S. Eliot, "Tradition and the Individualized Talent," in *Selected Essays: 1917-1932* (New York: Harcourt, Brace, 1932), 5.

64. For example, see Joyner's study of several North Carolina dulcimer makers, most of whom do not play the instrument themselves.

65. For example, see Dean Kimball, *Constructing the Mountain Dulcimer* (New York: David McKay, 1975), 55.

66. Ferris, 96. Glassie ("Artifact," 111) states that "in all things that man makes there is an aesthetic factor; there is no artifact totally devoid of art."

67. M.O. Jones, "Concept of 'Aesthetic,'" 77; Jones's discussion of folk-culture aesthetics should put to rest any charges that folk culture is deficient in aesthetics. See also Jones, *Hand Made Object*, especially 202-42, et passim. Jones has been the most outspoken champion of recognition for folk aesthetics, and other folklorists are now beginning to join in his call for more studies in this area; for example, see Toelken, 9.

68. Munro, *Arts and Their Interrelations*, 101. Kubler (66) states that "emotions function like a main valve in the circuit between us and the universe . . . the prerogative of artistic invention." See also Magda B. Arnold, *The Nature of Emotion* (Baltimore: Academic Press, 1968), for a good survey of the importance of the emotions in aesthetics.

69. Munro, *Form and Style*, 13. Toelken also notes (185) that the folk aesthetic "is usually unspoken, because it is functional not intellectualized."

70. Munro, *Arts and Their Interrelations*, 290.

71. For information about and illustrations of the zither and its possible affinity with the dulcimer, see Mercer, 482-97; Odell, "Folk Instruments."

72. See Franz Boas, *Primitive Art* (New York: Dover, 1955), 157, where designs are alleged to derive from dreams. See also M.O. Jones, *Hand Made Object*, 63, 250-51. Barnett (58) also discusses the idea but discounts it in favor of personal individual variations, and bricolage, as creative sources.

73. Barnett, 261.

74. Kubler, 69.

75. Glassie, "Take That Night Train to Selma," 38.

76. Barnett (101) notes that praise for originality and "ego-oriented experimentation" are more easily expressed in arts and crafts than in some other walks of life.

77. Ibid., 294.

78. Kubler, 82. Yet as Leonard Plotnicov states in "Creative Response to Customs and Traditions," *Humanitas* 7 (Spring 1971): 70, "people . . . generally regard customs and traditions as static entities and not as dynamic conditions."

79. Glassie, "Take That Night Train to Selma," 24.

80. Ferris, 96, 98.

81. Munro, *Form and Style*, 13.

82. M.O. Jones, "Concept of 'Aesthetic,'" 92; see also Jones, "Chairmaking in Appalachia," 286-88, 613-20. Toelken (185) asserts that "folk artists are likely to be fiercely aware of what is good and beautiful in their areas of expression."

83. See George Mills, "Art: An Introduction to Qualitative Anthropology," *Journal of Aesthetics and Art Criticism* 16 (1957): passim; see also M.O. Jones, "Concept of 'Aesthetic,'" 79, et passim. Yet as Toelken notes (9) too often folk-culture "scholars are likely to pay attention to the community standards for what a barn or quilt [or dulcimer] should look like, but they have been relatively hesitant to take seriously the aesthetic reflections of the performers [or craftsmen] themselves."

84. Munro, *Form and Style*, 11.

85. M.O. Jones, "There's Gotta Be New Designs," 58; see also Jones's "Violations of Standards" for a fine discussion of the roles customers play in affecting and even effecting elements of design and form through interaction with the creator. See also Plotnicov, who observes (76) that "creative responses are intimately related to social pressures."

86. See Lewis, 305. Lewis believes that the truly creative artist is not to be found in popular culture, which dotes on copying, conforming, fashions, and fads.

87. M.O. Jones, "There's Gotta Be New Designs," 59. Barnett (49) also discusses the possibility of "good and bad copies." In Barnett's terms, "good" ones would be (as Kubler says) replicas—such as Homer's—while "bad" ones would be mass-produced, factory, or assembly-line copies.

88. Munro, *Form and Style*, 15-16.

89. Clark E. Moustakas, *Creativity and Conformity* (New York: Van Nostrand, 1967), 32.

INDEX

active-passive bearers of tradition, 174
n.5
aesthetics, in folk culture, 2, 138-39,
147-56, 160, 164-66, 176 n.34, 180
n.40, 181 nn.66, 67, 68, 69; of handcrafted vs. machine quality, 75, 133;
Homer's, 2, 134, 144, 147-56, 164-66,
176 n.34; leading to change in
dulcimer, 38; and musical quality of
dulcimer, 83; and ornamentation,
91-92, 97, 99; and pegs, 103; and the
public, 140; in quality of wood, 53-54;
and traditional frets, 84-85
Alpine, Tennessee, 9, 123
Amburgey, Jethro, 19, 175 n.22
Appalachian culture, characteristics of,
9-10, 12-14, 16, 17, 40, 128, 141, 173
n.3, 180 n.48; stereotypes, 141

banjo, as folk instrument, 179 n.17
Barnett, H. G., 2, 159, 162, 179 n.31,
181 nn.55, 72, 182 n. 76
Barry, Phillips, 119
Berea College, 4, 21-23, 26, 31, 33, 43,
47, 146, 160, 175 n.26
bicentennial dulcimer, 159, 162, 163,
166-67
Bidstrup, Marguerite Butler, 18
bricolage, as creative process, 130, 158,
162-63, 181 n.72; examples of, 46, 69,
74, 105, 156, 158
Browne, Ray B., 178 n.10
buck-wing dancing, 173 n.1
Burrison, John, 144-45

Campbell, John C., 14, 21, 174 n.18
Campbell, Olive Dame, 16-17, 128, 174
n.18
Carter family, 29
copying, 32, 125, 127, 147, 182 nn.86,
87; of Homer's instruments, 41-43,
153; vs. replication, 124-25, 127, 134,
136, 138, 182 nn.86, 87
creativity and innovation: conceptions
of, 2, 130, 142-43, 144-47, 153-54,
159-69 passim; in Homer's musical
instruments, 32, 42-43, 48, 50, 65-66,
136, 145, 147, 160-70; in Homer's
procedures, 45-46, 65-66, 73-76, 93,
106-07; in Homer's tools, 32, 45-46,
65-66, 69-70, 76, 85, 93, 105, 129-31,
145, 158-59. See also Ledford, Homer,
inventions of
culture: analytic components of,
120-21; conceptions of, 2, 34, 113,
121, 177 nn.2, 3; 178 nn.10, 12; relationship with society, 2-3, 14, 34,
113-20, 137, 139, 141-43, 170, 178
n.12
customers. See Ledford, Homer, and
audience for craft

Dorson, Richard, 122
dreams, source of creativity, 158-59,
164, 181 n.72
dulcibro, 136, 170; as art work, 165;
creation of, 162-64; demands special
evaluation, 149, 159; description, 48,
50; as hybrid, 145, 162, 164